Ex Libris

Kindest regards of
Manly P. Hall

Manly P. Hall, Hand-Illustrated by Jessica Naomi

Manly P. Hall A Seeker of More Intelligent Life – Book Fourth

Compiled with graphics and edits by Darrell Jordan, Copyright © First Edition 2023. All rights reserved.

No part of this book may be reproduced in whole or in part without the written permission from the publisher, nor stored in any retrieval system or transmitted by any means, electronic, mechanical, photocopying, recording, or other, without the written consent of the publisher.

For bulk purchases, please contact the publisher.

Enquiry@Athenaia.Co

Library of Congress Cataloging-in Publication Data

Names: Hall, Manly P. | Jordan, Darrell

Title: Manly P. Hall A Seeker of More Intelligent Life – Book Fourth

Description: First U.S. edition. | Coeur D'Alene, Idaho: Athenaia [2023]

Identifiers: LCCN (pending) | ISBN 979-8-88556-046-7(First Edition hardcover)

Subjects: OCC040000: BODY, MIND & SPIRIT / Hermetism & Rosicrucianism, | PHI013000: PHILOSOPHY / Metaphysics, | SOC038000: SOCIAL SCIENCE / Freemasonry & Secret Societies

LC record available at https://lccn. loc.gov

On the internet: Parallel47North.com/collections/esoteric-books

Managing Editor: Darrell Jordan
Original Author and Essay: Manly P. Hall
Executive Producer: Yuka Jordan
Book Cover Art and Illustrations: Jessica Naomi
Image Credits: Manly P. Hall's personal collection
Printed and bound in the United States

Publisher: Athenaia, LLC
2370 N Merritt Crk Lp, Ste 1
Coeur D'Alene, ID 83814
The United States

Manly P. Hall

A Seeker of More Intelligent Life

Book Fourth

Darrell Jordan, MPS

CONTENTS

INTRODUCTION	9
NEW YORK, MAY 1937	11
THE SECRET DOCTRINE IN THE BIBLE	11
BIBLICAL COSMOGONY	13
THE GODS	14
THE FORMATION OF THE WORLDS	16
THE SEVEN DAYS OF CREATION	18
THE PRE-ADAMIC MAN	20
LETTER NO. 2	23
THE SECRET DOCTRINE IN THE BIBLE	23
ADAM AND EVE	24
EDEN AND THE ANGEL OF THE FLAMING SWORD	25
CAIN AND ABEL	31
LETTER NO. 3	36
THE SECRET DOCTRINE IN THE BIBLE -	
NOAH AND HIS WONDERFUL ARK	36
THE COVENANT	45
THE TOWER OF BABEL	46
ENOCH, ABRAHAM AND MELCHIZEDEK	48
LETTER NO. 4	49
THE SECRET DOCTRINE IN THE BIBLE - ISRAEL	49
THE WANDERINGS IN THE WILDERNESS	50
MOSES	51
MOSES RECEIVING THE TABLES OF THE LAW	53
THE TABLES OF THE LAW	55
THE TABERNACLE IN THE WILDERNESS	57
THE DEATH OF MOSES	62
LETTER NO. 5	63
THE SECRET DOCTRINE IN THE BIBLE -	
SOLOMON AND THE EVERLASTING HOUSE	63
SONG OF SOLOMON	68
PROVERBS	71
LETTER NO. 6	76
THE SECRET DOCTRINE IN THE BIBLE -	
THE GREAT MAN OF NEBUCHADNEZZAR'S DREAM	76
THE STORY OF SAMSON	78
THE VISION OF EZEKIEL	81
THE SUFFERINGS OF JOB	84
MELCHIZEDEK	87
LETTER NO. 7	88
THE SECRET DOCTRINE IN THE BIBLE -	
THE NEW TESTAMENT	88

THE BIRTH AND CHILDHOOD OF JESUS	90
THE MYSTICAL CHRIST	92
INTERPRETATION	96
LETTER NO. 8	101
THE SECRET DOCTRINE IN THE BIBLE - THE FLIGHT INTO EGYPT	101
THE CHILDHOOD OF JESUS	102
JESUS BAPTIZED BY JOHN	103
THE MARRIAGE FEAST AT CANA	105
THE RAISING OF LAZARUS	106
THE MIRACULOUS DRAUGHT OF FISHES	108
THE LORD'S PRAYER	110
LETTER NO. 9	113
THE SECRET DOCTRINE IN THE BIBLE	113
JESUS WALKING ON THE WATER	114
THE LAST SUPPER	115
THE GARDEN OF GETHSEMANE	118
CHRIST BEFORE PILATE	119
CRUCIFIXION	120
THE EMPTY TOMB	124
LETTER NO. 10	127
THE SECRET DOCTRINE IN THE BIBLE	127
THE PARABLES	130
THE PARABLE OF THE SEED	132
THE EYE OF A NEEDLE	133
THE GOOD SHEPHERD	134
THE PEARL OF GREAT PRICE	135
THE PRODIGAL SON	136
THE BEGINNINGS OF THE CHRISTIAN CHURCH	138
LETTER NO. 11	140
THE SECRET DOCTRINE IN THE BIBLE - THE JESUS OF PETER AND THE CHRIST OF PAUL	140
PAUL'S DOCTRINE OF THE LOGOS	144
THE MARTYRDOM OF THE DISCIPLES	145
BEGINNING OF THE CHURCH	149
LETTER NO. 12	152
THE SECRET DOCTRINE IN THE BIBLE - THE REVELATION OF ST. JOHN	152
CONCLUSION	161
AUTHOR AND MANAGING EDITOR	165
MANLY P. HALL BOOK SERIES	167

INTRODUCTION

EDITOR'S NOTE

Manley Hall was born on 18 March 1901, in Peterborough, Canada, to William S. and Louise Palmer Hall. The Hall family moved to Sioux Falls, South Dakota, United States, in 1904. Manly Hall later settled in Los Angeles in 1919.

As a young man, he became interested in all forms of occult subjects. He subsequently joined a number of societies, among them the Theosophical Society, the Freemasons, the Societas Rosecruciana in Civitatibus Foederatis, and the American Federation of Astrologers.

In 1922, Hall wrote his first book: Initiates of the Flame and was collecting all form of esoteric/exoteric/mystical subject matter, in his own words: "late in the fall of 1922, the plan for a comprehensive work on the symbolism of western mystical societies began to take shape in my mind. It soon became apparent that research facilities for such a project were not available in Southern California... The only answer was to contact antiquarian book dealers and elicit their cooperation in the search for the items desired." In 1934, Hall founded the Philosophical Research Society, a research institute modeled on the ancient school of Pythagoras.

He was ordained a minister in 1923 to an occult/mystic congregation at the Church of the People in California. In that same year specifically in May 1923, Manly Hall began the membership/student based, not for sale magazine, all written, edited and published by Hall titled the "The All Seeing-Eye."

We now follow Manly P. Hall from the "All Seeing Eye" book series at the age of 24, to his private lessons for his students in this latest book series, at the age of 32. In this series, Mr. Hall moves from imparting wisdom through stories to a confident, fact-based approach of his findings and understanding of his research. His elucidation exudes confidence and is well written, with it being exceedingly broad in scope. In this series we provide 4 years of lessons condensed into four books. We are positive you will find the information herein to be quite useful in filling in some hidden areas of understanding in religion and history.

Editing was minimal in terms of punctuation and spelling. In some cases, there are made-up words (or words that are no longer in use) in which case they were left spelled as is.

I'm sure that you will find, as did I, that Manly Hall was highly intelligent and possibly bordering on genius.

Suffice it to say, we are positive you will enjoy the many journeys Manly Hall takes you on.

Darrell Jordan, MPS

NEW YORK, MAY 1937

Dear friend,

THE SECRET DOCTRINE IN THE BIBLE

The Vedas, the sacred books of the ancient Aryan Hindus, appear to be the oldest of Scriptural, writings and the source of most of the sacred books now venerated throughout the world. The religious traditions of the ancient Hindus are of incredible antiquity. The traditions of these people indicate that the laws and institutes of the gods were revealed to the progenitors of the Aryans in the highlands of the Himalaya Mountain country nearly a million years ago. The migration of the Aryan tribes, first Southward and then Westward, resulted m the establishment of several sub-races and cultures. The migrating tribes carried with them the development of writing the records passed from the memories of priests and scribes to the more permanent and impersonal media of stone, clay and papyrus.

From the Vedas poured forth the streams of religious tradition which, flowing into various nations down through the ages, appear in the course of time as the single source of the numerous Scriptural writings of the world Great saints and sages interpreting this ageless wisdom, wrote their commentaries or restated in the terms of their own day the Vedic lore and the sacred tradition. In China, Lao Tze and Confucius were the interpreters and their writings have become Scripture. In India Buddha was the great Emissary. In Persia it was Zoroaster. In Egypt, Akhnaton and Hermes. In Greece, Orpheus, Pythagoras and Plato. In Syria it was Moses and later Jesus.

Bibles, so-called, are collections of inspired writing and the recording of ancient oral traditions. They are accumulated over immense periods of time and can usually be traced to the lore of preceding civilizations. They are built up from earlier fragments and should never be regarded as revelations in the sense of being, delivered in toto to any individual by some divine being. The revelation factor is generally limited to interpretation. Some illumined individual, contemplating sacred matters, perceives some deeply concealed value and by placing special emphasis upon this new aspect comes to be regarded as a religious founder.

Among ancient people, sacred writings were reserved for the contemplation of initiated priests and were not available to the laity. The priests interpreted such parts of the Scriptures as applied to the problems of the occasion. The populace, gathered before the temple, received their spiritual instruction from initiates of the priestly orders who stood upon the porch of the holy house and solemnly expounded the laws. These priests were equipped with the keys to the Scriptural allegories by which they were enabled to unlock the profounder parts of the spiritual tradition. After the decline of the Mysteries, the sacred books fell into the hands of the profane with the result that the subtler values were lost.

According to the teachings of the old initiates, the spiritual tradition was likened to a flame burning forever upon the altars of the gods. The flame was divided into seven flames and these in turn were again divided into seven, the result being forty-nine fires or the forty-nine spiritual revelations, called in the Cabbala of Moses the forty-nine gates of the law. Thus, out of the One Eternal Truth came forth the Seven World Religions, each in turn divided into seven lesser parts—altogether constituting the Divine Wisdom.

The Scriptures of the world are the written records devised to preserve and at the same time to conceal the secrets of the forty-nine branches of the Eternal Law. It naturally follows that there is a certain interdependence between religious writings. To understand any one sacred book completely, it is necessary to also understand all other sacred books. In spite of human prejudice to the contrary, there is but one religion and one truth and all the great faiths of the world are parts or fragments of the Ancient Wisdom. It has been difficult for human beings to accept this truth and for lack of interreligious understanding, there has been very little religious understanding. Each man, clinging to his own book, hugging to his heart his own fragment of the law, has believed that there is a peculiar virtue in proclaiming a part and denying the rest.

The Christian Bible is the principal sacred book of the Western world. It is usually divided into two parts and occasionally into three parts by the insertion between the Old and New Testaments of the Apocrypha or "doubtful books." The Old Testament sets forth the secret doctrine in Israel. It is a Cabbalistic book, almost unintelligible without the assistance of certain commentaries. The New Testament derives its teachings from the Essene mystics of Syria, the Mithraic cultists of Persia, the Seraphic Rites of the Egyptians, the Simonean Gnosis also of Syria, and the Neo-Platonism of Alexandria. It follows that the unknown authors of the Gospels were men learned in the comparative religious systems of their day. It is impossible at this time to engage in speculation or controversy as to the identity of the

Gospel writers. It is sufficient to say that they possessed a working knowledge of the Secret Doctrine and cunningly contrived to conceal this knowledge in what is made to appear as a historical narrative of the life and works of an individual.

We must concern ourselves with the Old Testament. Like the Christian revelation, the Mosaic tradition sets forth under the guise of history an elaborate metaphysical system derived directly from the older Egyptian lore and indirectly from Chaldea, Phoenicia and India. Moses was an initiate of the secret schools of Egypt, and the Pentateuch usually ascribed to Moses, is the surviving remnant of the most profound teaching. It is quite unlikely that the Pentateuch has descended to the present time in anything resembling its original form. In fact, there is considerable evidence that the true books of Moses were lost in the night of time. But whatever be the case, it is certain that although somewhat distorted in form, the Ancient Wisdom still survives in the Old Testament writings and can be extracted therefrom with the aid of certain keys and patient, illumined research.

Our interpretation of the Biblical writings is based upon a system of cross reference in which all the great schools of ancient religion and philosophy are considered as one composite structure. Thus, each system is interpreted in the light of the others. As each religion has been built up from innumerable older beliefs, the understanding of these various background beliefs is absolutely essential. The gaps in one system, where the tradition has been mutilated or lost, can be filled in from other systems of similar tradition. If the work's painstakingly done, the result is a complete picture by which the student is able to comprehend the correct meaning of obscure passages and fill in perplexing vacancies. The important thing is to be sure that the building is done from the same stream of tradition as the religion that is being reconstructed.

BIBLICAL COSMOGONY

The cosmogony of the Jews is derived directly from the Chaldean and Egyptian. This has been proved beyond any question of doubt by the discovery of cuneiform tablets much older than the Jewish Bible which contain many of the stories set forth in the opening chapters of Genesis. It is quite possible that the Old Testament originally contained a much more amplified account of the creation, but certainly it is still possible to make much more of the Book of Genesis than the average churchman has accomplished. With the aid of the Jewish and Cabbalistic commentaries, Genesis is amplified into a rational account of the beginning of the universe—far more vital, significant and impressive than the accepted theological version. A great scholar observed in the last century that Christian theology, and of course he included Jewish cosmogony, was the only system believed by the more advanced races of the earth to insist that God made the universe out of nothing.

THE GODS

The Book of Genesis opens with a simple and dramatic statement which has been Anglicized into the most impressive sentence in English literature:

"In the beginning God created the heaven and the earth."

This verse apparently presents no problem, but the more a searching student thinks about it, the more fully he will realize that into ten words has been compressed a cosmic process involving hundreds of millions of years of time and innumerable complicated mysteries. Only an elaborate commentary can make this verse even partly intelligible to the human mind entirely ignorant of divine and cosmic procedures.

We must first define the word GOD as it is used in this case and throughout the first chapter of the Bible. The word in Hebrew is not God or Jah or Jehovah, but ELOHIM. God is a reverent but entirely insufficient word to convey the true meaning of Elohim. Most important to be considered are two facts. First, in Hebrew, Elohim is an androgynous term inferring a combination of male and female attributes. Second, the word, by its termination, is plural. Actually, therefore the word ELOHIM means "the male-female creators" representing a host or at least a group of powers and not, under any condition, a single personal entity.

The words "heaven and earth" are also misleading, through inadequate translation. By heaven and earth should be understood a superior and inferior condition; a separation of qualities, not a division of place. The average reader will think "of heaven as the firmament and earth as the planet, and this interpretation will destroy entirely the significance of the verse. It would be better to interpret heaven and earth as spirit and matter, or the subtle and the gross in the sense of vibration or qualities of life and vitality.

The words "In the beginning" also present difficulties. The wise student will interpret them as "from that which is first" or "in eternal principles" or "that which was in the beginning."

This leaves only the word "created" and here again misunderstanding is almost inevitable. The human mind always thinks of creation as the making of something that is new. If we think, however, we will realize that in creating any physical thing, creation is only a new pattern made up of already existing factors. Thus, if a man creates a picture, he does so with the aid of paints and brushes and canvas, the true creation being the inward inspiration which applies these Instruments for the release of an idea. Creation in this verse implies rather formation, or manifestation, the arranging of ever-existing elements into new patterns to be the vehicles of purpose.

With these thoughts in mind, let us read again the verse according to a fuller understanding of its meaning:

From the eternal principles and essences, the androgynous creator-gods manifested forth the positive and negative aspects of Being.

Having thus clarified our interpretation, we can bring to bear upon it such commentary matter from ancient Jewish beliefs as will reveal the full significance of the verse.

The Jewish mystics recognized an eternal, definitionless Principle which they denominated AIN SOPH, the Boundless. From the Egyptians they derived the teaching that this Boundless One possessed three intrinsic aspects or attributes—Being, Life and Light. These three as one, and that ONE formless, ageless and changeless, was the true GOD whose most perfect symbol was SPACE—the source and ultimate of all things.

Periodically, according to great cycles, SPACE caused to emerge from its own nature, Primordial Unity—the objectification of Being, Life and Light. This first manifestation was called the Opened Eye and was designated by the Cabbalists KETHER, the Crown of the Eternal Glory. AIN SOPH, the Absolute, was life in suspension. KETHER, the first-born of the Absolute, was life in expression. Within the nature of Kether was manifested polarity, which is the foundation of activity. The polarities were called ABBA, the father, and AIMA the mother. Abba was the positive manifestation of spirit as force, energy, and power. Aima was the negative manifestation of spirit as matter, substance, and receptivity. From the union of Abba and Aima, that is energy and substance, was produced form.

According to the Cabbalists, the ELOHIM, or the creator-gods, were the progeny of the union of life and matter. It was the Elohim in turn, moving in Space, who brought forth the mundane universe over which they ruled. By mundane is meant not the physical worlds but the metaphysical system of which the physical creation is the lowest or seventh part. This first manifestation or agitation was equivalent to the conception of the universe in all its parts, or like the planting of a seed from which was to grow the worlds. It is the first motion in the Absolute.

The comparisons in other religious systems checks and justifies the speculations of the Jewish mystics. In the Northern Tibetan system, the meditations of Adi Buddha, universal consciousness, produces the seven Dhyani Buddhas or the seven modes of consciousness by which the world is formed. In the teachings of the Persians the Supreme Nature, Ahura-Mazda, manifested the Amesha-Spentas who become the Formators of the lower worlds. In the Egyptian Hermetic teachings, the Elohim are the Governors, the Cosmocratores. In the ancient Egyptian system, they were the Ammonian Artificers, the servants of Ptah who fashions the Egg of the Universe upon a potter's wheel. The ELOHIM are also the seven Cabiri of Samothrace; the seven rays upon the golden crown of the Gnostic Lion; the sacred seven, the unwritten vowels which together make up the name of the manifested divinity, the seven colors of the spectrum, the seven days of creation, the seven seals of Revelation. The eternity recurring septenary, by which art, music and physics are bound together, are the ELOHIM, the seven Breaths that move upon the Deep.

THE FORMATION OF THE WORLDS

The second verse of Genesis states:

"And the earth was without form, and void; and darkness was upon the face of the deep. And the Spirit of God moved upon the face of the waters."

Interpreted according to the mystical tradition, this would read:

And the below, the passive aspect of Being, was formless and devoid of manifested life, and darkness or oblivion filled the whole expanse. The spirits of ELOHIM moved, impregnated and enlivened the essences of the negative Principle.

In some of the Hindu works, this motion of the Elohim is referred to as the "curdling of Space" into the worlds. The seven modes of intelligence, which are the personification of the seven laws of nature, which are in turn the seven wills of the spirit, began to manifest patterns. They were first in the nature of vortices, called in the SEPHER YETZIRAH the whirlwinds. One form of this theogonic myth declares that the universe was created by the Deity speaking the Sacred Word. Of course, the Word was made up of the seven vowels of the Elohim which together are the Fiat which issues as a host of living powers from the "lips of the Creator in the North Asiatic tradition the seven Sons of the Eternal establish their foundation in the Deep. Seated in the six directions of space, six of the Builders turn upon the seventh who is placed in the center and is called the Immovable.

In the Cabbala, the center is called the Holy Temple, the Sabbath of eternal rest, around which moves the six days of creation. In the Cabbala the higher powers do not descend into the lower elements to ensoul the mundane diffusion, but rather cast their shadows upon the Deep or the lower elements. In the teachings of Eamaism we have a somewhat similar statement—the meditating Dhyani Buddhas dream themselves into the illusion of matter, causing a certain part of their own consciousness to assume the illusion of existence, though ever meditating above it. The shadows of the Elohim, descending into the depths of matter, result in the formation of four levels or planes of illusion which the old Jewish philosophers called "worlds."

These planes correspond roughly to the levels of spirit, mind, soul and body in man. In each of the four worlds, the seven Elohim are reflected, to become in all twenty-eight, which caused them to be associated in symbolism with the lunar month and its four weeks of seven days. The ancient Jewish priests had a peculiar veneration for the Moons, their faith being a lunar cult.

Only the lowest of the four "worlds" was involved in the physical creation. This lower or fourth "world"

was made up of seven parts or planes—the shadows of the seven Elohim. Of the seven planes which make up the mundane sphere, six are superphysical and one is physical, the lowest. The six superphysical are called CAUSAL and are the source of the energies and patterns which manifest or flow into and through the seventh.

The seventh and lowest diffusion of the fourth "world" is that with which the Creation story in Genesis is concerned. The unfoldment of this physical plane is according to the pattern commonly known as the Chaldean system of cosmogony.

In the cosmogony of the Greeks, the material universe is brought into being by seven gods, each of whom rules over one of the seven parts of the mundane diffusion. In the Greek system the gods are: Thanes, Ouranos, Chronos, Rhea, Zeus, Poseidon and Hades. The mundane world consists of seven interpenetrating spheres of which six are superphysical and the lowest or seventh is physical. According to this system, the seventh or physical plane is ruled over by Hades the subterranean god, to symbolize the physical plane as being the furthest removed from the divine energy.

THE SEVEN DAYS OF CREATION

The description given in Genesis I: verses 1 to 31, must be understood to represent the gradual development of the physical universe. The Elohim, the gods of the Dawn, mold the negative substances of being into the form and pattern of the solar system. Having brought the planets (including the luminaries) into objective existence, the Elohim then take up their thrones in the planetary bodies, and, according to the Chaldean genesis, circle about in their orbits age after age, governing with their celestial splendors the creatures of the lower world.

The pattern for the creation of our own solar system applies to all other solar systems in our universal chain. The pattern also applies to all forms of life evolving within solar systems, from suns and planets to grains of sand, electrons and atoms. This is the Cabbalistic teaching concerning the Macrocosm and the Microcosm, or the greater and the lesser creations, each patterned according to the other. This led the Cabbalists to say, comparing man, a microcosm, with the universe, a macrocosm, that "Man is a little universe and the universe is the Grand Man." This did not mean that the universe actually resembled man in his physical form but rather that the same system of geometry which patterned man also patterned the world, and that the same essences, principles and forces were in both. The Elohim say: "Let us make man in our own image" etc. That is, let the lesser creation be patterned after the greater creation, and be similar to it in principle.

Medieval theologians insisted that the seven creative periods called "Days" made up together a week similar in time to a week of mortal calculation. This the wisest of the ancient philosophers always denied, insisting that the term "Day" in Genesis referred rather to an age, cycle, or great period of time. Science uses such terms as "period" or "age" to signify one of the major divisions in the evolution of the earth and the life evolving upon it. Thus, such terms as the Miocene or Pliocene Age, or the Glacial Period. Modern science is of the opinion that the physical earth has existed for from 500 to 1000 million years. A recent discovery of fossil remains indicates animal life upon the earth at least 175 million years ago. When these figures are compared with the theological opinion that the earth was created by the arbitrary will of God in the 5th millennium B.C., it is apparent that science and theology come to a parting of the ways. The Biblical scholar, however, is not guilty of the delusions which afflict the pious but fanatical theologian who clings desperately to the jot and tittle of the "revised version." There is abundant confirming evidence to indicate that the Genesis given in the Bible describes processes occurring over a period of at least a billion years; and that it describes how the creative forces of nature brought forth sequentially the superphysical bodies of the solar system, then the material planets, and then shifting perspective to the planet earth, unfolded the life upon it up to the present state.

The descent of the Elohim with their hosts of spirits into the swirling mists of Primordial Substance and their molding of these mists into the sidereal patterns and bodies, constituted the involutionary process or the descent of spirit into matter. The unfolding of the worlds through the manifestation of ever-improving types of life, or the release of consciousness through a concatenation of improving vehicles, constitutes what Darwin called evolution. There is no real argument between science and religion. The difficulty is principally due to the extremely compressed description of the creative processes given in Genesis. If the reader can take such a statement as "And God created" and read instead: And the forces of nature, over a great period, caused to manifest—most of the difficulties will be overcome.

It should be distinctly realized that the ancients understood by their "gods" or creative hierarchies not personal beings performing sorcery in space but rather aspects of creative intelligence gradually unfolding through their own creations. In the Egyptian rites, it is said the gods impregnated space with themselves, and then the seeds of the divine natures sprouted and grew up to form the universe. The proper attitude is to realize that divinity is evolving in and through the universal formation. Evolution is really eternal life ideating or shining through material organisms, as a light might shine through a lamp. Evolution is also therefore inward life building ever more perfect forms through which to express its own potentialities.

The Book of Genesis, Chapter I, verses 24 to 26, inclusive, reveal that the ancients were fully aware of man's relationship to the animal world. In the sixth day, both the animal and the human kingdom is formed, the animal manifesting first and finally man, created in the image or likeness of the Elohim.

The first part of verse 26 requires special emphasis: "And God said let

US make man in OUR image, after our likeness." Then in the last part of the 27th verse it says: "male and female created he them." This is a very confused picture according to the King James version. That the word God is intended to be plural is evident in the statement, "Let us make man in our image, after our likeness." Here, of course, God should be read Elohim, the creators. By the word "said" in each case is to be inferred not to speak but to will or to inwardly determine, the same thought that is implied in the Tibetan creation when the worlds are formed by the meditation or the inward mental determination of the Dhyana's. In the Gnostic writings it is described that the Builders each gave to man a certain part of their own nature so that when he was finally completed, he participated in all of the universal powers and in addition possessed the life of the eternal Father, Ain Soph, the Boundless.

THE PRE-ADAMIC MAN

The condensation of the earth from its nebulous fire-mist state required many millions of years. In those ages, there was no time with which to measure the infinite processes, as time is man-made. At last, the body of our planet was formed and the surface of the earth was in a molten state, and vapors surrounded the whole planet. The earth was not habitable by any such creatures as man has recollection of, although it is taught in the old records that fantastic beings did float in the flames. The physical globe floated in a sea of superphysical humidity, termed by the Greeks "Æther." This is the origin of the primitive belief that the continents of the earth floated in a great sea. This Æther was not the physical humid vapors arising from the earth's surface, but vital ethereal element in which were evolving the forms that were later to descend upon the earth as species and races of living things.

Most of the ancient philosophies teach that life descended onto the physical planet from some sphere of superphysical energy which encloses the physical planet. Curiously enough this old opinion survives, and recent stratosphere explorations have discovered living spores in the stratosphere. A number of scientists have come to the conclusion that space may contain these spores which, like drops of condensing water, represent seed-lives oozed out of the etheric body of the earth. It is too soon to say what will be found in the opinions of scientists upon this matter, but it is also entirely too soon to declare the ancient philosophers to be wrong.

Boehme, the German mystic, describes the Celestial Adam who dwelt not upon the earth but in the heavens, a term which may infer this etheric diffusion. Certainly, the ancients believed that even the process of incarnation infers the descent of the superphysical principles of man from a humid sphere outside of the earth. This humidity is described by the old mythologists as a river which divides the earth from the outer universe. To the pagans this river was the Styx, and to the Christians it is the Jordan with its hosts of the Redeemed gathered upon the distant shore. The Greek poets wrote of the herds of souls floating in the mist which divides the world of the living from the world of the dead. By the world of the living is simply meant the physical plane, and by the world of the dead the superphysical, subjective universe, although in fact the opposite would be more nearly true.

In the Biblical story, man dwelt in a Paradisiacal sphere before his fall into the mystery of generation. This Paradisiacal sphere is called a garden and has been variously located by religious enthusiasts upon almost every part of the earth's surface. The fact, however, is that Eden is not on the earth's surface but above it, or, more correctly, in the higher etheric element which encloses the earth in a globe of translucent energy. The four rivers are the four streams of ether or energy which sustain the four kingdoms of the physical world—mineral, vegetable, animal and human. Man, physically is nourished by the vital ethers of nature. These ethers now work through him, but in pre-Adamic times, he possessed no physical body and these ethers formed an etheric body.

In the midst of Eden, was a small area which was termed Paradise. The ancients believed this to represent approximately the North Polar area of the etheric globe which, like the physical globe, possessed polarity. The study of cell life shows that impregnated cells develop first from their North polar caps, and the same is true of planets and all of the cosmic planes. The first connection between the etheric plane and the physical was polar. Therefore, physical life, moving downward from the etheric state, flowed particularly to the poles which were the first parts of the physical earth's surface to crystallize.

It is therefore stated that in ancient times, millions of years ago, the gods brought the seeds or germs of life first to the earth's polar cap. The descent of the gods is described in Genesis VI, 2, where the Sons of God saw the daughters of men and took unto themselves wives. By this we are to understand that the cooling of the earth's surface resulted in the liberation of elements. These elements, moved by the will of the gods, gradually assumed forms and patterns, even as the impregnated cell gradually builds an organism capable of sustaining individual intelligent existence.

In the very ancient times, the first bodies were such as air and water, for these responded most easily to the impulses of the creating will. When the vehicles or bodies built up first from the more subtle parts of the physical globe reached a certain degree of development, the spirits dwelling in the ether above and called in the Bible the "Sons of God," flowed downward and into the new bodies which are called the "daughters of men" or more correctly the daughters of Manas or mind—the mind—formed bodies—for the word man literally means mind.

While dwelling in the Paradisiacal state, the entities which we now know as men were androgynous, as is explicitly stated—"they were created male and female." In the old Cabbala they are described as having been formed back-to-back, a male and female organism. But more correctly is to be inferred that they possessed inwardly the potentialities of both positive and negative powers.

The Edenic Garden contained not only the rudiments of human existence but also the other kingdoms which were to manifest. It was therefore a sort of superior earth in which forms of life developed and prepared themselves for physical incarnation, even as the wise in this world are building superphysical bodies in which to function when the race has finished its physical evolution.

The name given to the order of life which was to incarnate as human was ADAM which means species, type or kind. Never for a moment does it infer a single individual. Adam, therefore, correctly means a mode of consciousness, a type with mind, as distinguished from the animal and vegetable kingdoms which do not possess individualized intelligence, and therefore are properly termed species. These lower kingdoms have a center of consciousness called a monad, whereas man has evolved his monad into an ego or a center of "I am-ness."

The process of man's entry into physical existence, or the birth of the terrestrial Adam, was preceded by an elaborate evolutionary program. Forms were built up in the material world by a process of natural experimentation. These forms were not habitable by creatures possessing mind and they passed away in the laboratory of evolution. It was only after hundreds of millions of years of growth and development that forms were generated suitable to the manifestation of the celestial Adam.

The forms which were not used, called the mind-less, the shadows, and the monsters, are described by Berosis in his Chaldean history as composite beings made up of animals, birds and fishes with many heads. They are also referred to in the Cabbala as the Kings of Edom, the unbalanced giants who perished in the Void. In chapter VI, 4th verse of Genesis it says: "There were giants in the earth in those days."

At last, by the workings of nature from below upwardly, forms were organized through which the human life wave could come into manifestation. When this process had been consummated, man's consciousness descended into a specially prepared part of what appeared to be the animal kingdom, whereupon this kingdom branched off definitely from the true animal kingdom, resulting in the scientific perplexity concerning the missing link and the origin of human individuality.

Such are a few of the reasonable conclusions, sustained by the ancient commentaries and cosmological systems, to be derived from the early chapters of Genesis.

Yours very sincerely,

Manly P. Hall

LETTER NO. 2

Dear friend,

THE SECRET DOCTRINE IN THE BIBLE

Part II

We have already suggested that the story of Adam and Eve as given in the opening chapters of Genesis is an allegorical exposition of the cosmic processes which resulted in the differentiation of the human species.

It is important to realize that the secret doctrine concealed in the Bible must be discovered with the aid of certain keys. Each of the myths, fables and symbolic figures has at least seven complete and distinct interpretations. In other words, to open the door, that is unveil the secret, the key must be turned seven times in the lock. In the ancient Mystery rituals, the key was an important emblem of discovery or enlightenment. Neophytes received symbolic keys as Part of their investures. In the Mithraic Rites candidates were taken through seven doors, which they unlocked; and in the Egyptian Mystery of the resurrection of the soul, the aspirant was brought to the gates of fulfillment and was interrogated by the keepers of the gates.

It may seem strange that one story or account may have several meanings, but such is the working of the Cabala. In the original Hebrew, there were numerical and letter cyphers to aid in the decoding of the hidden information. Translation and editing have destroyed these older Cabalistic patterns, and it is now necessary to have recourse to the fascinating field of comparative religion in order to unlock the Biblical secrets.

ADAM AND EVE

As an example, ADM (Adam) is, first of all, species or kind, meaning a particular generation or genre. ADM is also a symbol of Adonai, the creating Lord. ADM is also Aries the first sign of the Zodiac; ADM is the incarnating ego, the father of the multitudes; ADM is the human principle perpetuated forever in the seed; ADM is again Protogonos, the ideal or archetypal pattern, Plato's Idea or Logos; ADM is the universe "whose body nature is, and God the soul." ADM is the first race of humanity and, by analogy the first sub-race of each of the following races; ADM is the sun; and also, in the story of the Garden of Eden, the typical neophyte seeding initiation into the Mysteries. This one symbol indeed plays many parts. The First Man becomes the figure of all first things. Of the sciences, he is mathematics; of forms of knowledge, he is pure wisdom; of religions, he is the esoteric tradition itself. As we develop this subject, we shall try to show you how all of this is true.

It is also important to remember that nearly every personality described or discussed in the Bible is primarily a symbol and not a historical individual. It is a great mistake to believe that there is great spiritual virtue in the perpetuation of history or the worship of ancestors. The virtue lies not in the accepting of the sacred writings but in the discovery and application of the ever-living truths secretly hidden in the Scriptural books of the world.

The creation of Adam is described in Genesis 2:7. The Creating Power formed man "of the dust." In the Cabala, this man is called Adam Kadmon or the species formed of the red earth. The meaning of red earth in this sense is most obscure, but certainly has no reference to physical soil. In a cosmic sense, the universe is fashioned of a fiery nebula, and the whirling fire-mist from which the Cosmos was formed is the red earth.

The ancient writings, in describing the generation of the physical bodies of the animal and human kingdoms, declare these vestments "coats of skins" to have been exuded from the auras or superphysical bodies of a divine race which dwelt in space, i.e., the earth's outer atmosphere. This teaching requires considerable explanation.

Man consists of three parts or natures. The first is the divine principle, a spiritual substance identical with spirit and space. The second part is a sidereal nature, sometimes called the soul, and constitutes a superphysical body—the "luminous chiton," the garments of glory, or aura. The third part is the sublunary nature, the objective body with its several systems—muscular, arterial, glandular, etc. Man as Spirit dwells in the substance of the One, or undivided from the Divine Principle. In the Bible, this state of identity with the Supreme is expressed by the statement "abiding in Abraham's bosom." This has the same meaning as the Samadhi or Nirvana of the Eastern metaphysicians. At the beginning of the Day of Manifestation—that great cycle of time figured in Genesis as the Seven Days of the Formations—the innumerable natures of living things emerge from the Original Unity, and "God" becomes "the gods;" whereas the Cabala expressed it, "the multitudes emerge from the simple unities."

This emergence of the gods is their descent into the state of individualized living things. The Primordial Sparks robed themselves in the "luminous chitons" or superphysical bodies. The gods are therefore described as spheres of light, and of this order of beings is man himself—inwardly a divine nature participating in the Supreme Effulgency. This is explained in the Bible by the placing of spiritual humanity (Adam—Eve) in the Paradisiacal sphere called Eden. Here souls dwelt garmented only in light and truth, the auras, as yet undefiled by contamination with physical matter. The records of this ancient time are preserved in the mythologies of all classical civilizations. It is beautifully described in the Gnostic Hymn of the robe of glory wherein the paradisiacal state is represented as the homeland or fatherland which all exiled humanity is seeking. With this key the mystery of Eden is easily unlocked.

EDEN AND THE ANGEL OF THE FLAMING SWORD

The Adamic being is given dominion over the Garden, always a symbol of the astral world, what Levi the transcendentalist calls the astral or magical light. The same illusion to the garden occurs in the story of Parsifal.

Here, Klingsor attempts to delude the Knights of the Grail by creating a magical garden filled with the enchantments of the senses. In some of the ancient books, the universe is called a garden and the planets and suns are flowers blossoming in space. With Adam (the human life wave) abides also the seeds and germs of the several other kingdoms. In Genesis 2:11, the Creating Power fashions the animal kingdom. The intellect of Adam "named," that is examined and understood, all the creations.

The next important allegory relates to the creation of Eve, the female or negative principle. To understand this, we must realize that the original Adamic Man, that is the spirit in its luminous vestments, was in itself androgynous According to the ancient Jewish legends, Adam was formed with two faces and two bodies united back-to-back, that is with two natures, each facing in the opposite direction. In the Authorized Version, the Creating Power is said to cause a deep sleep to descend upon Adam and from his side Eve was created, Genesis 2:21:23. Eve is the etheric principle called by Plato the principle of generation. This is exuded out of the auric body in the same way that the hard shell of a snail is exuded from the soft substances of its body. The etheric vehicle or the feminine principle, as it is referred to in ancient times, is described in Genesis as being the tempter. Lack of true understanding as to the meaning of the "temptation" and the "fall" led Christian theologians to regard all female kind as the embodiment of temptation and corruption. In fact, the old story to the effect that "with Adam's fall we sinned us all" is one of the most ludicrous errors of theology. Nowhere is it more evident in Scriptural writings that "the letter of the law killeth" than in this particular instance. In fact, the whole Christian theory of redemption and the estate of Christ in the concepts of orthodox theologians, depend upon the literal and benighted misunderstanding of the ancient Chaldean myth, long regarded not only as history but as Scripture.

The 3rd chapter of Genesis opens with the description of the serpent and contains the account of the Temptation and Fall of the "first man." The old Jewish Mysteries declare the serpent to be a symbol of Samael the archangel of Mars, and the master of the astral light. In Scriptural writings, serpents are frequently used to represent currents or waves of force moving in space. The Midgard Snake of the Nordic Eddas and the Orphic serpent twined about the Egg of the Year are both symbols of the Zodiac and the serpentine course of the sun. The erect serpent of Egypt and the hooded Naga of India and Cambodia signify the spinal fire in man. The winged serpents of Gobi and the Taoist dragons of China represent both the psychic forces of the soul and the initiates or sky-men. The Indians of the Southwest of America have serpent symbols of similar significance, and the Quetzalcoatl or Feathered Snake of Central America is a symbol of the initiated or high priest. The Druid priests of Britain and Gaul called themselves serpents, and these are the snakes that St. Patrick's said to have driven from Ireland. The reader of the Bible should be acquainted with these facts, for it is only depth of scholarship and breadth of understanding that can interpret correctly the serpent symbol in Genesis. The astral light over which Samael has dominion is the sphere of imagination and desire. In the Cabala it appears that Samael is the adversary, yet in the Authorized Version there is no explanation for the existence of the tempting serpent or why the all-wise Creator should have placed it in the Garden to corrupt this noblest work of God—man.

The key to the riddle lies in the metaphysics of the Persians which in turn was derived from the most ancient religious Mysteries of both the Near and the Far East. It is explained that good and evil so-called are but the aspects or qualities of One Principle. For example, creation brings into manifestation the innumerable hosts of lives which lie sleeping in the Infinite. In this respect creation is release or expression and therefore good. But creation also infers certain limits and boundaries being placed upon space. Thus, the very world which is man's sphere of opportunity is also his living tomb and, in a sense, therefore evil or adverse to the luminous inner self that must dwell so long in the fetters of matter. Every action therefore of the creating power is described as bringing into manifestation not only a good but an evil spirit or angel.

A simple example of this is the modern problem of invention. Whenever a man invents some new and useful improvement, to make life more secure and comfortable, abuse inevitably follows. Good laws are perverted by selfish men; great ideals are brought down to a thousand purposes inconsistent with the original dream. Primitive men realized this and the earliest scriptures teach that the universe is a battlefield of good and evil impulses which they termed "gods" and "demons." Even as God was the Chief and Lord of all the benevolent forces, so the evil agencies or negative attributes are personified in one offending being variously named Satan, Lucifer, Yama, Loki, Hades, Kali, etc.

In the 3rd chapter of Genesis, the adversary is Samael, the Serpent, and like Mephistopheles it is "a spirit of negation; part of the power that still works for good while ever scheming ill."

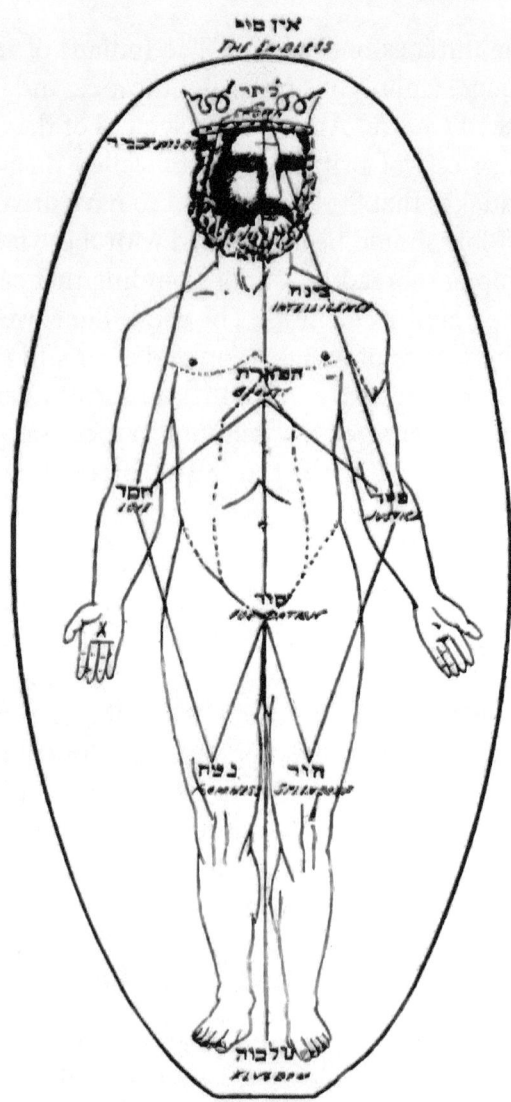

CABALISTIC FIGURE OF ADAM

IN THIS DIAGRAM ADAM-KADMON, THE FIRST MAN, STANDS CROWNED WITH THE CELESTIAL GLORY. ON HIS BODY ARE THE SYMBOLS OF THE TEN WORLDS OR EMANATIONS. FROM THE FIGURE WE ARE TO UNDERSTAND ADAM AS COSMOS, OR THE ONE LIFE, MANIFESTING THROUGH WHAT PYTHAGORAS CALLED THE DECAD OR DECIMAL SYSTEM. IN THIS SYMBOL ADAM IS HIMSELF A FIGURE OF THE TREE OF LIFE. THIS INTERPRETATION GIVES A NEW AND RICHER MEANING TO THE BIBLICAL ALLEGORY OF THE FIRST MAN.

In the Pythagorean formula, unity alone is perfect wisdom, for wherever there is division desire is born. Desire is only possible under a concept of diversity, for possession is one of the first of the illusions. Desire leads to an innumerable array of other evils and is itself rooted in ignorance which in turn is man's inability to perceive the sovereign Oneness of all things.

The chapter further explains that there are two trees growing in the Garden of Eden. One is the Tree of the Knowledge of Good and Evil, and the other is the Tree of Life. The symbolism of the tree must also be briefly explained. The World Tree is the earth's axis and occurs in nearly all ancient mythologies. Trees are also symbols of evolution and unfoldment because all life, tree-like, emerges from one root and seed and extends itself into a diversity of manifestation. The Cabalistic Tree of the Sephiroth's with its ten symbols is based upon the Tree of Life in the midst of Eden. The tree is also the symbol of racial development and nearly all forms of evolution are even now diagrammed under the form of a tree. So also, are genealogical systems. The tree becomes the symbol of continuity. Special trees have particular symbolism, as the pine tree of Atys which has become the modern Christmas tree, and the Cedars of Lebanon which was a title bestowed upon an order of ancient priests. According to one derivation the word Druid means tree and the dryads were the tree-spirits of the classical Greeks. All these interpretations are significant to the present subject. But there is another even more immanent in its inferences. There are two great systems in the body of man: the tree of life which is the arterial with its roots in the heart; and the tree of the knowledge of good and evil, i.e. the nervous system which has its roots in the brain. These two "trees" are physical manifestations of a complicated network of branching energy currents in the aura or superphysical bodies.

In medieval art, it was customary to represent the Tree of the Knowledge of Good and Evil in the form of an apple tree. In fact, this fruit has been concerned with two important episodes in the history of man. There was the apple that Eve ate and the apple that fell on Newton's head. These two apples have changed the course of history. The older mystical writings show not an apple but a pomegranate, and Greek statues of Kore and Persephone frequently depict these fertility goddesses holding pomegranates. This fruit also had a place in the rituals of the Eleusinian Mysteries and seems to be the original of the Chaldean "apple."

Madame Blavatsky in ISIS unveiled showed that the 3rd chapter of Genesis was part of an ancient Mystery ritual representing the drama of initiation into the higher grades of the esoteric school. In the Cabala, Adam is described as attending a school of the angels in heaven. It was in this celestial academy that the first man received the keys to that secret doctrine which has descended through an unbroken hierarchy of initiated priests since the first dawning of human consciousness. The angel Raphael visited Adam and Eve in the Garden and discoursed with them concerning the mysteries of the soul. According to Madame Blavatsky, the disobedience of Adam and the eating of the forbidden fruit represented an effort to secure the esoteric wisdom without being properly and duly initiated. In other words, it was a violation of the laws of the Mystery Schools, an attempt to storm the gates of heaven. For this violation, primitive humanity was exiled from the spiritual state and the symbolic Fall occurred.

By another interpretation equally significant, the serpent tempter represents the intellectual principle. This is evident from the words of Jesus in the New Testament, "be ye wise as serpents." The intellectual principle leads to the experience of conscious self-responsibility. This is exile from the Edenic garden of innocence or spiritual infancy. The evolving intellect of primitive man brought with it a gradual extroversion. From an inward contemplation of spiritual principles, man came to recognize an external life. Slowly the inner senses were dimmed and the perceptive powers correspondingly strengthened. The result is man's present state in which he has little if any inward life and is entirely over conscious of the significance of outward circumstances. The inner life is the Paradisiacal or Edenic state. The outer life is the relapsed or fallen state. The resurrection promised by the Messianic dispensation is the restoring of the inner life and the conquest of the external or sensory sphere. All this is clearly shown in the Buddhistic teaching and is an essential part of the Platonic dicta.

The Creating Power in its aspect as the laws of nature now pronounces a curse upon the disobedient mortals. They are doomed to the cycle of birth and death. They are no longer supported and sustained by the inward light but must struggle to survive in a universe of doubts and fears. Ixion is bound to his wheel, and the cycle of necessity has gained dominion over the divine spark—the hosts of Adamic souls.

In Genesis 3:21, it is described that the Creating Power fashioned for Adam and Eve "coats of skin." These are the physical bodies—the mortal vestments of immortal life. Man's memory of his heavenly state is obscured by the world of matter and he is cast forth from the abode of peace. At the gate of Eden, the Creating Power placed Cherubims and a flaming sword to guard the sacred Garden that Adam and his progeny might not return to it again. It is interesting that Solomon, when he built the "everlasting house" should have placed upon the doors of the temple Cherubims with the flaming sword. This is the hey to the whole mystery. Eden is the first Holy of Holies. Its significance is identical with that of the Adita of ancient temples. It is the heart, the sacred place. It is also symbolic of the state or condition of sanctity. The temple is not a building but a state of consciousness, an inward realization. He who attains to this realization enters the holy place which is guarded from the profane by the keepers of the gate—the testers or initiators. Philo Judaeus declared the Cherubims to represent clouds or obscurations which conceal Eden from the profane. These clouds are the ignorance, benightedness or perversion of the unredeemed which must forever obscure sacred things.

CAIN AND ABEL

In the 1st verse of the 4th chapter of Genesis, Eve says, "I have gotten a man from the Lord." The ancient Jewish Mysteries declare this to mean that Cain was the child not of Adam but the archangel Samael, the serpent, the mysterious luminous power at the root of all human perplexity. In the Authorized Version the translation is so obscure that both Adam and the Lord are referred to as the fathers of Cain, but the early rabbin's knew their Scripture better than 17th century theologians, and the old commentaries insist that Cain was the son of Samael, and Abel was the son of Adam. Cain was therefore the embodiment of cosmic fire and Abel the son of the agrarian principle. It was for this reason the Chasidim explained that the offering of Cain was not acceptable to the Lord, leading to the first crime—the murder of Abel. That this story also relates to the Mystery rituals is evident from the words of Voltaire that the Samothracian Mysteries were the account of a brother slain by his brethren. Early efforts were also made to identify the drama of Osiris and Typhon with the Abel-Cain story. The murder of Abel is one of the most difficult of the allegories to interpret, but in substance the story is as follows:

If we understand Adam to be man, the incarnating ego, the one father of all the bodies that are manifested by an entity during its life cycle, we will realize that by the FALL is described the descent of this egoic vortex into the sphere of generation. It first produces phantom forms in the astral light, a progeny of demons by Lilith as explained in the ancient Commentaries. Later by union with the humid principle, Eve, it begins the generation of bodies, this mystery cunningly concealed under the genealogy or the descent of the Patriarchs. In the process of generation, polarity must first be established. In the Chinese cosmogony, which by esoteric interpretation is also anthropology, the creation arises from the endless strivings of two principles termed YANG and YIN. In the Greek system, Æther and Chaos are the polarities from the mingling's of which the Cosmos is fashioned. As the physical universe is engendered from the opposing of polarized forces, in like manner the soul arises from the strivings of the polarized will and by an alchemy within the consciousness itself.

Jacob Boehme, the German theosopher, depicts this striving within the Self by a series of symbolic figures showing the eternal battle between light and darkness, between action and inertia, wisdom and ignorance, etc. Later, Johann Gichtel illustrated Boehme's principles with a series of curious engravings, now extremely rare, but the best mystical key ever prepared for the interpretation of the Scriptures.

Cain and Abel represent the first discord or confusion arising in the superphysical organism of man. It is evident that the allegory has universal application or it would not be part of the Mystery rituals of many ancient orders. Furthermore, it is a known fact that all these rituals relate to the unfolding of the human soul, so Cain and Abel must be some part of the consciousness of man. Boehme creates the terms "divine will" and "self-will" with which to designate the two parts of man's consciousness which are ever in a state of mutual striving. The allegory of Lucifer and his battle with Michael the Archangel has similar interpretation, the war in heaven being merely the conflict within the soul or superior nature as contrasted to the body which is the earthly nature.

It is evident that in this allegory Cain represents self-will or the active principle and his descendants became builders of cities (bodies) and workers in metals (the sense perceptions). Tubal Cain, described in Genesis 4:22 and who later occurs prominently in the Masonic allegory, first, pounded swords into ploughshares. Here, he represents self-discipline as an aspect of self-will by which the destructive emotions are refined and tempered. The descendants of Cain were all wanderers and artisans and of the race of builders, and in the 23rd verse of chapter 4, it seems that the crime of Cain is repeated by Lamech his descendant. A study of this chapter will show that in the cycle of the Patriarchs the principle of recapitulation is ever present. In the same way, Noah is a second Adam.

This is explained by the Chinese who declare that the cycle of existence is represented by the Zodiac. At the end of each great age of manifestation, the universe is dissolved in the sign of Pisces, or the Deluge, and is reformed or reborn in Aries. Aries is the sign representing Adam, Taurus is Eve, Cain and Abel are the twins or Gemini. The Eternal Principle is reborn at the beginning of each cycle, even as it is stated definitely in Genesis that Adam was not the first man but merely the first man of the cycle, or an incarnation of the Eternal Man, the Protogonos of Plato. In Genesis 1:28 the Law (Lord) said to Adam: "Be fruitful, and multiply, and replenish the earth." This is exactly the same thought expressed in the ancient Confucian metaphysics. All creation is a replenishment in space, a new manifestation of eternally existing principles.

If we realize that the signs of the Zodiac are the Patriarchs even as later, they are the Prophets and the Apostles, we shall perceive that creation so-called is the movement of the Ego or consciousness, whether microcosmic or macrocosmic, through the twelve signs or parts of the SOULar year. This SOULar year is the Manvantara of the Hindus, the Day of Brahma, the flowing of the Great Breath. This Breath is also mentioned in Genesis 2:7 where the Law (Lord) breathed into the nostrils of Adam the breath of life. There is much commentary material in the Zohar, the Hebrew Book of Splendors, concerning the significance of the Great Breath, but only a suggestion is possible in the space at our disposal.

If, then, Cain and Abel are the light and dark halves of the human will, born like Castor and Pollux from the single Golden Egg, the Ego, we can understand why the Greeks symbolized the soul as a sphere made up of a gold and a silver hemisphere pinned together. We know that in the ancient Mystery temples, certain disciplines were given for the perfection of the human soul. The Ancient Wisdom was disseminated throughout the East and the Near East by means of ritualistic dramas called the Mysteries. Lao Tze the Chinese sage, as librarian of the Chou Dynasty, read the ancient books brought to China from India. We are told also that Osiris, the great leader of the Egyptian faith, was brought from India in the form of a golden bull. This is again a reference to the Secret Doctrine having been brought from Asia and circulated throughout Mesopotamia and the Mediterranean civilizations.

Eastern metaphysics (and the Jewish religion is Asiatic) are based largely on the glorification of the passive principle. In the Hindu books we learn of the sage who, by sitting quietly under a tree, discovered by inward contemplation what all the strivings of the outer life could not attain. Lao Tze taught the sovereign dignity of doing nothing. You have to do nothing very intelligently and profoundly, however. It is not superficial laziness that is a spiritual virtue but rather a perfectly enlightened inward tranquility that can come only with the mastery of all external forces and circumstances.

Abel, in the allegory, brings his offering, the "firstlings of his flock" and offers them to the Law. By these are meant the animal propensities of his own nature. Such is always the meaning of the burnt offerings referred to in the Scriptures. Because he brings the "animal" his offering is accepted. Cain, on the other hand, brings the fruit of the ground and this is not accepted. The fruits here represent not principles of the soul but merely the consequences of action. Cain's offering represents the same type of superficial gift that the rich man gives when he presents a stained-glass window to the church but continues to cheat the widows and orphans. Cain gives of what he has, for fruits represent accumulation or possessions; but Abel gives of what he is, the "firstlings," his transmuted animal nature.

Cain, incensed, slays his brother, reminding us of the words of the Indian classic, "the mind is the slayer of the real." Thus, the allegory has an eternal significance. It is the very fey to the whole Mystery Religion. It is the reason why most faiths are today empty of esoteric wisdom. It is the fey to that ceremonialism of the superficial life which obscures the inward perceptions and brings creeds down to a useless war of sects and bigotries.

The 5th chapter of Genesis is devoted to the genealogy of the Patriarchs from Adam to Noah. It will be observed that in this chapter there is no mention of either Cain or Abel. Seth therefore is established as the founder of the races of the earth, begotten in the image of Adam his father, even as in his turn Adam was begotten in the image of the Lord—the creative hierarchy. Much has been made by Biblical students of the extraordinary length of life attributed to the Patriarchs. In chapter 5, verse 5, Adam's age is given 930 years, and in verse 27 Methuselah is recorded as living 969 years. It should be understood that these numbers are Cabalistic and refer not to the span of individuals but the duration of families, clans and blood records. Also, in the Jewish system of metaphysics, each of the numbers is symbolic of certain Hebrew letters. These letters form words according to the ancient hieroglyphical system attributed to Moses. The proper decipherment of these symbolical "ages" reveals the astronomical and cosmological import of the Patriarchs and their lives.

Realizing that Adam is not an individual but the human life-wave, it follows that his children and their children unto the tenth generation are the branching's and forcings of the racial tree; also, the differentiation of the cyclical currents by which the life of man and the life of the world are sustained. This explanation solves such problems as arises in Genesis 4:15, where the wife of Cain is mentioned, yet the Scriptural accounts infer that at that time Cain and Abel were the only progeny of Adam, supposedly the only man in the world. Also in the same verse Cain builds a city which he names after his son. One man could scarcely build a city nor could the abode of one man be termed a city. But when we realize that Cain is a race, we then understand that the story of his wanderings is an account of racial migration.

By Seth is to be understood a new generation, one which takes the place of the earlier creation that had failed and destroyed itself. An account of this earlier race is to be discovered in both the Chaldean and Chinese writings. The historian Borassus describes the monsters that were formed in the primordial ILUS, the slime-born, the monsters with many heads, a strange order of prehistoric COMPOSITA which vanished away in the dawn of time. In the GNOSTIC REMAINS it is described that the Demiurges, or creating power, fashioned innumerable bodies while experimenting with the cosmic substances. Most of these bodies were incapable of containing a mind. They were the night-born, the false birth, the monsters of the Abyss. This account is based upon the Hermetic legend, wherein it is described that these first creatures were destroyed by the gods because they could not be the vehicles or bodies for the incarnation of intellectual entities. Of such an order also are the giant-kings of Edom who "perished in the void." Also, these are the Sheddai, the antediluvian kings recorded in the Zohar. The third of the children of Adam, Seth is the third race known in the occult tradition as the Lemurian.

It was in the later sub-races of the Lemurian race that the human being we know as man was differentiated from the animal prototype. Thus, in Lemuria the true man came into being. Man having been formed as the vehicle for the "thinker" we have the explanation for the opening verses of chapter 6. The 1st verse describes that men began to multiply on the earth; and in the 2nd verse it explains that the sons of God (the intellectual egos or conscious entities) gazed upon the bodies that had been formed (the daughters of men) and took wives from among them, i.e., joined with them to become the true humanity that we know. Thus, Seth is the physical archetype of man, even as Adam is the spiritual archetype of man.

Sincerely yours, MANLY P. HALL

LETTER NO. 3
THE SECRET DOCTRINE IN THE BIBLE

Dear Friend,

Seth occupies a most important place in the order of the Patriarchs. Seth is the first of the perfect men. According to the Cabalistic interpretation of the Bible there were thirteen men born perfect. The inference is that in the end these thirteen will be the Messiah and his twelve disciples. There appears to be a direct reference to this mystery in the words of Christ, "Before Abraham was, I am" and "You were with me before the worlds were." The thirteen perfect men represent the flowering of the ages. In each order of descent of the Patriarchs there is one who is perfect. The first is Seth and the second is Noah. It is written in the Talmud that Noah was born with white hair, a strange prematurely aged creature whose father was so vastly amazed at his appearance that he hastened to his guide and counsellor the ancient Methuselah, saying, "What manner of offspring or son is this?" Methuselah replied, "He is the one who is to bring the oblivion, therefore thou shall name him Rest or the Suspension that is to hang above all things." Therefore, the child was named Noah, which means rest or that which moves not and is suspended above the oblivion. Noah is the tenth descendant from Adam, and Noah is the son of Lamech, and Lamech is blind.

In the line of descent from Cain, every fifth Patriarch is a murderer. In the case of Lamech it is written that he was blind and used to hunt with the aid of his son, a small child. This child, perceiving a strange object at a distance and thinking it to be an animal, pointed his father's arm, so that Lamech shot the creature and it fell dead. But upon approaching, they discovered they had killed a human being. The little boy explained to his blind father that the man who lay dead before them had a horn in the middle of his forehead, whereupon Lamech fell to his knees in great anguish and cried: "I have slain my own ancestor Cain!" for the Lord had placed a horn upon his forehead that every man should know him.

NOAH AND HIS WONDERFUL ARK

The sixth to ninth chapters of Genesis inclusive are devoted to the story of Noah and his Ark. In order to understand this story, it is necessary to have recourse to the early Jewish commentaries. As Noah is the second

Adam, he becomes the foster father of the human family, according to the Jewish metaphysical system. Also, Noah, preserving the just according to the will of the Lord, was a prototype of Christ, for as Noah saved his family and carried them over the Deluge, so in the Messianic tradition the Messiah is made to carry the souls of just men over the Armageddon at the time of the destruction of the world.

In the most ancient writings, Noah's Ark is not called a boat. Its name signifies some peculiar form of enclosure, a superior place to which men could go for refuge. The idea of a boat floating on the water was a poetic figure developed by later theologians. It is merely a symbol of the spiritual world which survives the disintegration of the physical universe. We can say briefly that the Ark of Noah, with its three decks, represents the three parts of the divine sphere. The Ark's a miniature of the universe.

Cabalistically, the Ark is shown to be the Zodiac, the Grand Body containing all the animals and seeds of living things. The key to the whole story is the Ptolemaic system of astronomy. In the night of the cosmic oblivion, the seven spheres which make up the lower creation are dissolved one by one and are absorbed back into the cosmic substance. The first to be absorbed is the earthly sphere, then the lunar, then the Mercurial, then the Venusian, then the Solar, then the Martial, then the Jupiterian, and lastly the Saturnian. As explained in the Greek mythology, Saturn in the end eats up all his children. This means that during what the Hindus call Pralaya, or cosmic night, the lower worlds sleep and everything that is below the Zodiac rests in a state of chaos. The Ark is therefore, the Zodiac which rides securely upon the face of oblivion.

According to the ancients, the mundane universe is enclosed by a crystalline sphere of stars called the angelic world. This sphere is divided into three parts according to the same rule still employed in astronomy. There is a Northern hemisphere of stars and a Southern hemisphere, and these are separated by an equatorial belt called the Zodiac. These three parts of the heavens are the three decks of the Ark; they are also the three sons of Noah. The mast which Noah placed in the midst of the Ark is the polar axis. According to the Talmud, Noah took into the Ark three hundred and sixty-five kinds of reptiles and thirty-two major divisions of animals. As the serpent was the symbol of the year, the three hundred and sixty-five reptiles are the days and the thirty-two major divisions of animals are the thirty-two paths of wisdom described in the Cabala. These paths consist of the ten Sephiroth's and the twenty-two letters of the Hebrew alphabet.

There are some fragments of the Noah myth not very well known to modern Bible students. According to one of these there was an animal called the reem that was too large to get into the Ark. In order that it might be saved, Noah tied a rope to the animal and allowed it to swim behind the vessel. This legend is derived from the same source as the Hindu account of Vishnu, who assumed the form of the Great Fish and pulled the Ark through the sea by a rope fastened to his back. As all the principles of life are enclosed within the Ark, it is necessary for the principle of matter to be there also. Therefore, we learn from the ancient Jewish writings that at the time of Noah there was also upon the earth a very good giant who was named Og, king of Basham. As Og was too large to get into the ship, he is depicted in the ancient Cabalistic figures as sitting astride the roof being fed by Noah through a small hole or window.

It was most necessary that the Deluge should accomplish precisely its purpose. For this reason, the ancient writers go into considerable detail in describing how the oblivion was brought about. There were giants upon the earth and if the waters came from below, the giants were strong enough and numerous enough to close the fountains of the earth. If the waters came from the heavens above, these same giants were so tall that the earth's surface could be inundated and they would still escape. To solve this problem, the Elohim caused the substances of the Deluge to flow first through the sphere of Gehenna and thus to descend as a Mazing deluge upon the place beneath, destroying all things. From this account it is evident that the ancient Jewish rabbins did not consider the Deluge to have actually consisted of water, but by the term water inferred rather cosmic substances.

According to these same rabbins, the "water" of the Deluge was both male and female. This was because part of the waters descended from above the firmament and pap came up from the Abyss. The two streams then mingled in Gehenna and flowed forth upon the temporal earth. The male and female waters are those described in the first chapter of Genesis as the waters which were above the firmament and the waters which were beneath the firmament. To release the upper waters, which caused the Deluge, from the firmament, Jehovah Elohim removed two stars from the constellation of the Pleiades, and to stop the flood he replaced them by taking two stars from the constellation of the Great Bear. In a previous lesson, we learned that the sign of Taurus represents Cain, therefore the Pleiades, which are in this constellation, are the children of Cain and thus we discover a key to the reason for the Deluge. The two stars borrowed from the Great Bear are guardians of the Pole and represent the reestablishment of order or the repointing of the polar axis.

When the flood subsides, the Ark is said to rest upon Mt. Ararat. Ararat is the Polar Mountain, the Olympus of the Greeks, the Meru of the Hindus. It represents the first firmament or the heavens which are above the earth, that is the sphere of the fixed stars. Remember that Saturn is the chief of the Elohim in that he is the eldest of the seven planets or Chaldean gods. It is Saturn who says in the beginning: "Let there be a firmament in the midst of the deep."

When the first day of manifestation, or remanifestation, begins, the Saturnine principle of crystallization dominates space and the firmament is manifested. Mt. Ararat, upon which the Ark finally rests, is the foundation of the new creation, the first sphere of the renewal of life. It is therefore represented as a high peak, but it has nothing to do with the physical mountain by that name in Syria. When the Ark has come to rest and the Holy Spirit or breath of life in the form of a dove, is sent out, the new day of manifestation begins.

From these suggestions and interpolations from various sources, it becomes evident that the story of Noah is far more complicated and far more interesting than might first appear from the Bible account. It is therefore now necessary to interpret this allegory with the keys supplied by the secret doctrine. The Ark of Noah symbolizes primarily a box or a container, and this is the clue to the whole interpretation. The sacred Ark or Argha occurs in the esoteric teachings of many ancient peoples. The Ark of the Covenant containing the sacred relics was carried by the Jews throughout their wanderings in the wilderness. A similar Ark was venerated by the Egyptians who depicted it in bas relief on the temple at Philoe. In the Egyptian legend of Osiris, the body of this god is sealed into an ornamented box which is set floating upon the river Nile. Deluge stories are to be found in the mythologies of all ancient civilized peoples. For the most part these accounts have been either completely rejected by modern science as fabulous or else entirely accepted as literal history. The possibility of a secret or allegorical meaning has been for the most part ignored.

In Jewish metaphysics, it is taught that superior principles reflect themselves into the material world, casting their shadows, as it were, into the substances of the Deep. This is according to the Hermetic law of analogy, which declares that those things which are below are like unto those things which are above. By this rule, the spiritual nature of man is reflected in his corporeal structure, the body being the shadow of the soul. Every part and member of the body, every function and process taking place within it, bears witness to cosmic laws, eternal in the heavens, that is existing forever in the superior nature.

The Ark is the symbol of the seed. Metaphysically, this seed, in the case of man, is a spiritual vortex containing within it the germs or roots of his mental, emotional and physical natures. The seed, reflected downward, becomes by Hermetic analogy the physical body itself within which, as within a chemical retort, the alchemical processes of life take place. The physical man is therefore a unity, or one living creature suspended from a unity—one spiritual entity. The body is the physical manifestation of recondite and superphysical agencies, fashioned "like unto its cause" and "bearing witness unto the law." Plato refers to the body in one place as like unto the shell of an oyster, and in another place, he calls it the sepulcher of the soul. This sepulcher, sarcophagus, or burial chest, is also the Noahite Ark.

The thoughtful student will therefore realize that the account of the Deluge has two widely different meanings, one relating to the sphere of causes, and the other to the sphere of effects. The thoughtful mind can never cease to admire the rare skill with which the ancient Scriptural writers incorporated many meanings into a single script, that the Book itself, like the truths for which it stands, might be actually "all things unto all men."

We have learned that Adam is the spiritual causal man, the "higher face" of the microcosm, "the most ancient of the most ancient ones," the ever-existing Self. We have learned that Noah is the second Adam, that is the reflection of the eternal Self in the substances of the transitory universe. Metaphysically speaking, Noah is the incarnating ego in its aspect as father of the three bodies which emerge from its own nature and constitute together the human personality. The three sons of Noah are the mental, emotional and physical principles. Their wives, or as the Hindus call them, Sakti's, are the physical correspondences—the brain, the heart and the reproductive system. Thus, we have a complete pattern: Noah, the incarnating ego; his wife, material essence itself; his sons, his emanations; their wives, the physical foci which these emanations set up. All is contained within the aura itself—the Ark, or as the Hindus call it, the Ego.

It is written that Jehovah Elohim, angered at the evils existing in the world he had fashioned, determined to destroy his creation, but, that the principles of this creation might not vanish with it, he caused the one just man and his family to build the Ark, take into it the forms of life, and float in security above the Oblivion. This means:

First: that at the dissolution of the universal system the principles of life are withdrawn from the material sphere and retire into the cosmic seed, or germ, which rests securely in space until the gods refashion the worlds.

Second: that at the end of a great wave of evolving life upon the earth, as for example humanity, the human principles retire into their spiritual counterparts and "rest" until a new order of bodies are created for them to inhabit in the next world cycle.

Third: that at the end of each physical incarnation the superphysical principles of man retire into the Ego, there to rest in the after-death state until the incarnating principle builds a new body, a new heaven and a new earth, when these principles emerge again in the mystery of birth and growth.

But we have said that the allegory has two distinctly different meanings. The second cycle of interpretation is that by which the Ark becomes body rather than seed. It is stated in the Apocalypse that for 42 months the Gentiles tread over the outer court of the temple. It is also stated in this same work that for 42 years, periods, or eras of time, the seven-headed serpent shall have power to blaspheme. The 42, a most mysterious Cabalistic number, is generally concealed under the round term 40, even as the number 70 in the Old Testament always actually infers 72. Jesus fasts for 40 days and 40 nights in the wilderness even as Noah floats for 40 days and 40 nights through the Deluge. Cabalistically, this fact identifies Noah and Jesus as both being personifications of the same principle. Cyphers are frequently ignored in certain forms of the Cabala. Thus the 144 thousand in Revelation becomes merely 144 or 12 times 12, referring to the Zodiacal cycles. The 40 days of Noah therefore becomes 4 cycles or periods; by one key the 4 races which make up the involutionary cycle or the cycle of descent ending with the Atlantean or fourth root race.

The Ark's the mundane universe in which the souls of men and of all living things are locked or sealed during the involutionary process. The outer world or temporal existence is symbolized as a chaos. Man is a spiritual entity living in the material universe as light surrounded by darkness. He is a cosmos floating in the chaos. He is potential wisdom surrounded by ignorance, that is by the sphere of the unknown. The 40 days of Jesus in the wilderness represents the travail of the human soul achieving realization; and the 4 cycles of which it is a symbol are the sufferings and travail of humanity seeking to establish order, peace and security in the phenomenal world.

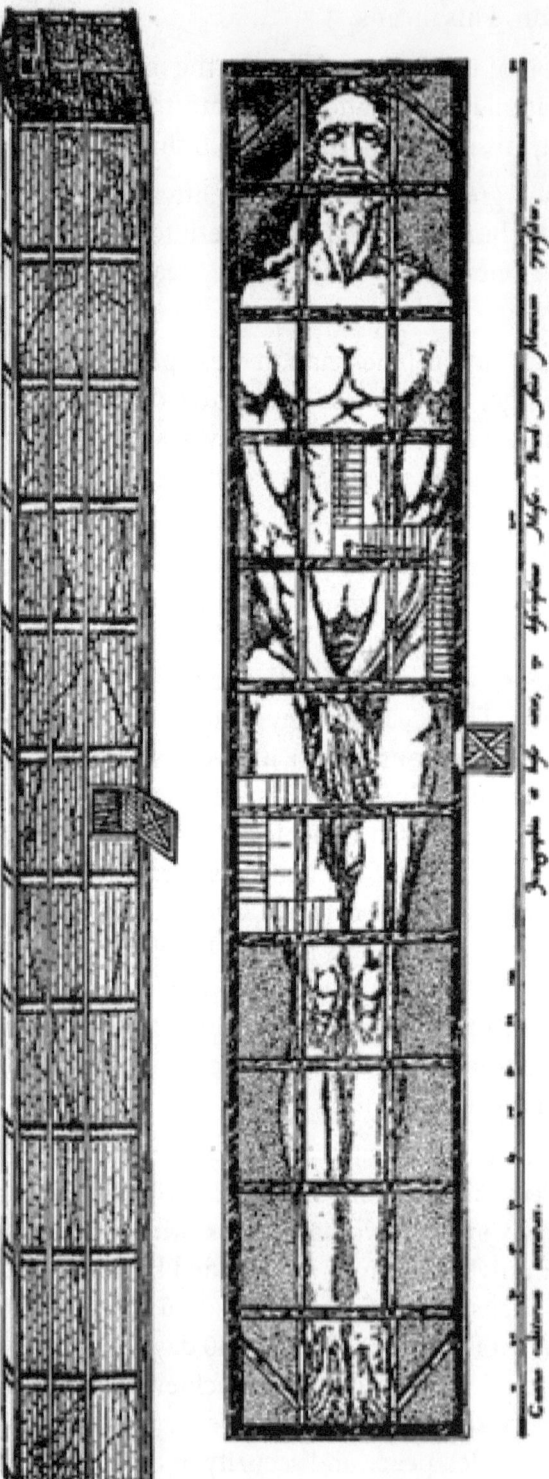

NOAH AND HIS WONDERFUL ARK

IN THIS RARE AND CURIOUS CABALISTIC FIGURE, THE ARK OF NOAH IS SHOWN TO BE SYMBOLIC OF THE TOMB OF CHRIST. THE FIGURE OF NOAH LYING IN THE ARK HAS THE NAIL WOUNDS IN THE HANDS AND FEET TO SHOW THAT HE IS A TYPE OF THE MESSIAH. HERE ALSO IS THE GREAT FIGURE OF THE ZOHAR SLEEPING THE NIGHT OF COSMIC REST, VISHNU ASLEEP ON HIS COUCH OF DARKNESS. IT IS THE CREATING POWER WHICH HAS WITHDRAWN ITS PRINCIPLES BACK INTO ITS OWN NATURE—ITS EMANATIONS SYMBOLIZED BY NOAH'S SONS AND THEIR WIVES IN THE BIBLICAL STORY.

According to the Cabala, Noah carried the body of his ancestor Adam into the Ark and when the Deluge had subsided reinterred the body on the hill of Golgotha. Of course, this is a mystical fable by which is arcanely set forth the esoteric truth that all forms or bodies, of which the Ark a symbol, carry within them the primordial germ, the root or seed of species and races. Adam, not as a person but as a type or life principle, lives eternally in its progeny or creations and is the true germ of fertility by which all things are made fruitful. Adam continues in its offspring even as all causes continue in their effects or are made manifest through them. In the Greek mythology, there is a descent of deities from the first and eternal Principle which is denominated Unaging Time. In the mundane order, that is in the hierarchy of gods controlling material universes, Unaging Time the Primordial Principle is manifested through Zeus who is termed the son or offspring of First Cause. If we consider the primordial Adam to be a symbol of the eternal principle of life, then Noah like Zeus becomes the mundane manifestation or direct descendant of First Cause. For this reason, the Cabalists refer to Noah as the second Adam, the foster or secondary father of the races of the earth.

If we see the Ark as a figure of the physical universe, then we understand how all living things are grouped together in one small vessel with three decks, the measurements of which are entirely symbolical. We also understand why this strange ship should have but one window, a problem which has perturbed agnostics no end. The Chinese signify the material universe as ruled over by an ogdoad or hierarchy of eight principles—Khwan and Kheen, the male and female potency which combine in six combinations called the sons and daughters. This account belongs to the most ancient of the Chinese sacred books the Yih-King or Classic of Change. Confucius wrote an elaborate commentary upon this work, which he declared contained the secrets of the whole universal emanation.

Poets have likened man's terrestrial state to an exile in a desert land—humanity cast away on a little globe in space surrounded by an inconceivable infinity. In the Jewish metaphysics, the Ark's are planet or the solar system floating in a sea of cosmic space, its decks crowded with the complex genera of living things. Thus, the Deluge myth is part of the story of the Fall of Man, told differently but still retaining for the wise its secret import.

In the microcosm, the Ark, being the human body, contains within itself innumerable living powers. During the prenatal state, the embryo floats ship like in the sea of the amniotic fluids. At birth, the individual organism is launched forth upon the stormy sea of life beset with its innumerable perils, Cabalistic ally represented by the forty days of the Deluge. Noah harkened to the voice of the Lord, that is he lived according to the Law, perfecting his soul and enriching his consciousness with the many experiences which result from the mystery of living. As a consequence, the "Lord" protects the life of Noah and brings the Ark at the end to a safe resting place upon the Mount of the illumination—Ararat. Part of the thirty-third degree of Freemasonry includes an interpretation of the symbolism of Noah and his Ark. Considered mystically, the story of the Flood is the wise man's mastery of adversity. It is the philosopher surviving the onslaughts of ignorance. It is the illumined mystic floating safely over the chaos.

Other interpretations should also be considered. Some ten thousand years before the beginning of the Christian era, the Island of Poseidon is, the last remnant of the great Atlantean Empire, disappeared beneath the surface of the ocean as the result of a terrific natural cataclysm. The records of this destruction have survived as tradition and form part of the legendary history of most ancient races. Plato had received the account of the sinking of Atlantis from the records left by Solon. He realized that the historical Atlantis offered a magnificent opportunity to combine history with philosophy. Plato was an initiate of the Eleusinian Mysteries. It was forbidden by this Order that any of its initiates should openly reveal the secret tradition. So, Plato cunningly concealed in his account of Atlantis the metaphysical doctrine of the initiates concerning the Fall of Man and the constitution of the human soul. The loss of the prehistoric empire was used to veil the fall of the angels. Atlantis, with its vast population, became symbolical of the etheric sphere that descended into the humidity of generation. The sea swallowing up a great race was the sea of matter swallowing up the hierarchy of human souls at the beginning of the mundane cycle of manifestation. It is only necessary to compare Plato's account with the Pythagorean system of mathematics to discover the correct key. Also, the city that consisted of alternating zones of land and water arranged in concentric circles was no material community but the solar system itself as can be easily seen by anyone who cares to diagrammatically draw out Plato's description.

As Plato used the history of the lost continent to veil the secret of man's lost spiritual state, so likewise did the Hindus, Chinese, Chaldeans, Mayans and Jews. There can be no doubt that there is a direct relationship between the story of Noah and the lost Atlantis, but what most writers have been unable to discover is the relationship between both Noah and Atlantis and a third metaphysical tradition.

Noah, born with white hair and prematurely aged of course, the symbol of mind, or that which is above the confusion of matter. Noah is the Knower. As Noah is the intellect, so Og, king of Basham, the good giant, is the personality or body consciousness, as we learn from the interpretation of the cyclops myths of the Greeks. By another interpretation Og is the oversoul or Anthropos, the one-eyed giant who is too big to go into the body—the ark but sits on the roof, that is dwells in the upper parts of the aura and is fed through the one small window, the pineal gland or third eye. There is also a legend to the effect that there is a baby born in the Ark. This is the soul which is born from the chemistry of the body and is identical in its significance with Harpocrates, the infant god of the Egyptians described in the Osirian cycle. The infant is therefore the celestial Self, the Christ within, born amidst the animals, for the Ark of Noah and the manger of Bethlehem are identical in meaning.

THE COVENANT

The 9th chapter of Genesis describes the Covenant between Noah and the Elohim. The symbolism of the rainbow is extremely obscure. In Genesis 9:13, the Elohim Jehovah says: "I do set my bow in the cloud, and it shall be for a token of a covenant between me and the earth." Among ancient peoples, the rainbow was regarded as a bridge connecting heaven and earth. In the Norse mythology, this is Bifrost. Up this bridge of light, the Ases climbed to the royal place of Asgaard. The seven colors distinguishable in the rainbow were sacred to the creating gods and from the earliest time the priestcrafts distinguished their ranks and offices by the color of their garments. Even in the Christian church, certain colors are associated with the saints and the persons of the Godhead. The Gnostics related color and sound, assigning one of the chromatic tones to each of the vowels. As the white light of the sun contains within it all the colors of the spectrum, so the Divine Effulgency, the eternal light of God, though in itself colorless, contains the spectrum of the creating principles or gods which emerge from it and become the Formators of the worlds.

It cannot be supposed that the ancient peoples were entirely conversant with our modern scientific concept of light and color, but they did associate the seven colors with the planets, the worlds, the invisible heavens, the orders of angels, and the aspects of the Divine Nature. The rainbow is therefore an appropriate symbol of the divine power. In it were visible together the colors of the seven worlds. The appearance of the rainbow at the end of the Deluge appropriately symbolized the releasing into manifestation the energy of the Logos through its seven principles—the Builders of the cosmos.

The reestablished universe, according to the Cabala, is divided among the sons of Noah who therefore become symbolical of the creative trinity. To Shem is given the center of the world, or, according to the Chaldeans, the central band of constellations, i.e., the Zodiac. To Japheth is assigned the Northern part of the world and the Northern constellations. To Ham the Southern extremities of the heavens and the earth, of the parts and members of the Grand Man of the Zohar, Shem receives therefore the heart as his throne or dominion, and Japheth the brain. To Ham is given the generative system. Thus consciousness (Shem), intelligence (Japheth), and force (Ham), are the creative triad remanifested after the Oblivion. Ham is called the dark one because he represents the physical universe, and the dark earth which is its most appropriate emblem. From Shem, Japheth and Ham descend the races of humanity, and to this newly. established human kind is given the collective term Israel. The word Israel signifies not the Jew in particular but all humanity, and the evolution of man in the period subsequent to the Atlantean Deluge is symbolically described by the wanderings of the twelve tribes of Israel. These tribes are the twelve orders of human beings dominated by the signs of the Zodiac.

THE TOWER OF BABEL

In the ancient Hebrew language, the word which is translated "ladder" can also mean a hill, a mound or any artificially contrived means of ascent. It is quite possible therefore that the Jews used the term ladder to include the type of building now called a pyramid. Most early illustrations of the Tower of Babel show it to be the type of building called by the Chaldeans a ziggurat, or astronomical observation tower. The ziggurat was an artificial hill with a circular ascending stairway moving in a spiral around the outside. Of such type of buildings, some ruins still remain and reconstructions of the Hangring Gardens of Babylon invariably show this type of structure. The Tower of Babel, as described by the Jesuit priest Athanasius Kircher, was undoubtedly an astronomical tower. The building was said to have been erected by the descendants and servants of the ancient hero Nimrod who was called the mighty hunter. This building, built of mud and held together with slime, was the prototype of Jacob's Ladder which led up through the seven worlds to the sphere of the Zodiac. The story of the Tower of Babel has many meanings:

1. It is a form of the World Mountain—Asgaard, Meru, Olympus, the Axis Mountain of the ancient Egyptians, the symbol of the North Pole.

2. It is the Mystery School or philosophical ladder, the rungs of which are the degrees of initiation. Man, climbing upward through the sacred stations of the initiatory rite, was declared to be ascending toward the gods. The levels and platforms of the ziggurat were appropriate symbols of the planes of consciousness through which the human soul ascends toward Reality.

3. The Tower of Babel is the physical earth itself. The ancient ziggurats nearly always had seven steps of six platforms rising from a foundation. The foundation in this case is physical matter and the six ascending platforms are the superphysical parts of the earth's septenary.

4. The Tower of Babel is man's own seven-fold body, the organism through the perfection of which he becomes "as a god, knowing good and evil."

5. The Tower of Babel was physically and actually an astronomical monument. The Magian star-gazers ascending this tower and examining the stars were said to be communing with the gods.

In the Biblical account Babel is man's monument to pride, and in the end, the gods confused the tongues of men and prevented the completion of the tower so that the word Babel has come to mean a confusion of tongues. The original word was a form of Babylon. The confusion of tongues is symbolical of the corruption of the ancient Mysteries and the intellectual darkness which descended upon ancient man as a punishment for the perverting of the sacred rites. The secrets of the esoteric wisdom were lost and, as in the Greeks mythology, the gods punished mankind for its presumptions and vanity. The Jewish story of Babel is of the same type as the Greek myth of Prometheus. But it was while studying the stars from the heights of Babel that the Chaldean star-gazers discovered the sacred alphabets of constellations which later recur in the account of the handwriting on the wall of heaven at the feast of Belshazzar. The Hebrew alphabet is composed of letters based upon star groups. For the sacred alphabet, the student should consult Gaffarel's unheard of curiosities concerning the TALSMANIC MAGIC OF THE PERSIANS.

ENOCH, ABRAHAM AND MELCHIZEDEK

Accounts differ greatly as to the exact time at which Enoch lived. According to some opinions, he lived before the Deluge and inscribed the wisdom of the prehistoric world upon pillars which survived the destruction of Atlantis. The Greek philosopher Solon, visiting Egypt in the sixth century before Christ, claimed to have seen and examined these pillars in a subterranean temple upon the bank of the Nile. In the Cabalistic legends, Enoch—the second messenger of God—was one of the Messianic gods or perfected men. He did not die but ascended to heaven walking with God. The most significant part of the story of Enoch is the Apocryphal account of the building of the "Royal Arches." With the aid of his son Methuselah, Enoch is said to have created a subterranean temple. This consisted of several rooms, one above the other, each with an arched ceiling. Descending from one room to another in the heart of the earth, Enoch placed in the lowest of the arched chambers a golden triangle with a secret name of God inscribed thereon. After the translation of Enoch, the site of his temple was lost and for centuries men sought in vain for the secret room, later, when Solomon resolved to build the everlasting house upon Mount Moriah, his workmen when digging the foundation discovered the sealed-up vaults of Enoch. Solomon s temple was therefore built upon the site of the mysterious temple with its seven arched rooms.

In Freemasonry, the symbolism of the Royal Arches of Enoch is carefully preserved. The whole temple is an astronomical mystery. The seven rooms, one above the other, represent the orbits of the planets. The golden triangle concealed in the lowest room is man's own triform divinity, or threefold Ego, the principles of will, wisdom and action, hidden in the dark substances of the material world. By one interpretation, Enoch is the human spirit itself, the builder of the seven bodies or arches, for the spiritual part of man is the only part which "walks with God" and does not know death.

Abraham means "A Brahman" and seems to refer to an importation of Oriental philosophy at some remote time in the history of the Jews. Abraham comes into the presence of Melchizedek, and at their meeting is the first record of the ceremony of the Eucharist. It is commonly believed that the word Melchizedek means "king of righteousness" but this is an orthodox version at the expense of accuracy. Melchizedek actually means "hail to" or "honor to" or "power to Sedek." Therefore, the name can be freely translated the authority of Sedek or Sedek is king. Melchizedek, Prince of Salem, really means then Sedek is king of Salem. The word Sedek is Egyptian. Sedek was the father of the Artificer gods of Egypt. The seven planetary gods called the Cabiri are the children of Sedek. Melchizedek therefore is the father of the planets, or, astronomically the Sun. Like Moses, the red-haired man whose name is also a Cabalistic title of the Sun, Melchizedek is the great orb of heaven, therefore his own father and mother and the founder of the eternal priesthood. Later Christ is called "the Light that lighteth every man that cometh into the world." Christ is therefore a type of the spiritual sun, the light-bearer, the light-bringer, called by St. Paul a priest forever after the Order of Melchizedek. In other words, a priest of the Sun or of the Solar Mystery or of the Eternal Light.

Sincerely yours,

Manly P. Hall

LETTER NO. 4

Dear Friend,

THE SECRET DOCTRINE IN THE BIBLE - ISRAEL

The word Israel is used in Genesis 50, v. 2, as a synonym for the name of Jacob. This verse reads: "And Joseph commanded his servants the physicians to embalm his father: and the physicians embalmed Israel." In the Cabala, there are seven keys to the meaning of Israel. Of these, the historical is the least significant. The word literally means "God is a warrior." In Genesis 22 is described Jacob's wrestling with the Angel. The Angel blesses Jacob and says, in the 28th verse, "Thy name shall be called no more Jacob but Israel." From this, it is evident that the accepted translation of the word is hopelessly inadequate. The true meaning of Israel is the objectified power of God—the divine power as manifested through the universe—of which the heavens with their stars is the highest visible part.

The cosmological key reveals that by Jacob we are to understand the sphere of the fixed stars—the same celestial world which Pythagoras calls the Parent of all terrestrial things. In the Greek mythology the starry heavens are called Argus, god of many eyes. These eyes are the Archangels and the celestial hosts, for it is written that "the eyes of the Lord run to and fro throughout the whole earth." The word earth in this sense means the world or the universe. Jacob or Israel, being the whole of the starry heavens, his immediate progeny are the twelve Israel great constellations which form the Zodiacal belt. In the Biblical allegory these are figured as the twelve Sons; in the Cabalistic teachings, the Zodiacal signs are the origins of twelve great streams of life which, flowing through all parts of creation, fill the world with their progeny. The stars are the race of heaven, the population of the firmament, and they are ruled by kings greater than any kings of the earth, even the kings of Edom—the Lords of the stars. When we think of Israel, therefore, we have not only to consider a people or a tribe or nation but of the whole life of nature, the gods of heaven whose shadows are upon the earth.

The second key to the mystery of Israel interprets the fable anthropologically. The twelve heavenly races in the sky are reflected upon the surface of the earth as the twelve tribes of Israel. The common notion that the twelve tribes of Israel make up the Jewish nation is quite incorrect, as Israel means all life and the tribes of Israel are all living things. Israel is a generic term for humanity as a collective whole, regardless of race or nation. When this collective humanity is signified by a single term, it may be called Adam or again Jacob. Both represent humanity. This is in the same sense that we use the word man to signify either one man or all men.

THE WANDERINGS IN THE WILDERNESS

The opening chapter of Exodus is devoted to an account of the oppression of the Jews in Egypt. Here again history becomes the instrument of a secret metaphysical tradition. Egypt is not a country in this account but a condition of consciousness. The story of the wandering of the twelve, tribes is identical in meaning with the account of the Prodigal son who took his patrimony and went down to spend it in the fleshpots of Egypt.

Natural processes are accomplished by two cosmic motions. One of these is termed involution or the descent of life into form. In this process, units of radiant energy take upon themselves ever more of the material elements until they are hopelessly obscured by the forms with which they have surrounded themselves. This state is typified by the seed, the hard shell and the living germ within. The second cosmic motion is evolution. This is life releasing itself from form by the process of growth. It requires billions of years for the cosmic plant to grow up, but by the evolutionary process all things are ultimately released from form and are restored to their divine state.

The bondage in Egypt represents evolving life at its nadir. Involution has reduced the spiritual monads or germs to a condition of complete impotency by enmeshing them in material elements. Physically this corresponds to the period in the evolution of life when nature consisted entirely of monocellular organisms. Gradually over a vast period of time evolution released through these cells, the entities which we now term plants, animals and men. The wanderings of the twelve tribes therefore represent the ages of growth and development, the slow and painful courses of evolution.

The third key to this ancient allegory is truly mystical. The human soul in a state of complete materiality is in bondage in a land of darkness. Man searching for truth, humanity collectively searching for truth, is well represented by a nation wandering in the wilderness searching for the promised land. The promised land is always happiness, security and the end of strife. It is the Nirvana, the peace which results from accomplishment. The Exodus of Israel is in part at least an ancient initiation ritual depicting vividly the liberation of the human soul from bondage to its animal desires and appetites and those creature comforts most men live for.

This perspective enables us to approach the story of Moses with a fuller appreciation of its metaphysical significance.

MOSES

The life of Moses is most obscure if considered historically, but recourse to the numerous Cabalistic legends and interpretations reveal clearly the place of Moses in the drama of the ages. The true name of the prophet will probably never be known for the word Moses is a title not a name. It is merely a rearrangement of the three Hebrew letters which form the word Shemmah which means the Sun. In China the Zodiac is called the Yellow Road, and the Sun is called the Emperor of the Yellow Road. Moses, in relationship to the twelve signs of the Zodiac, has a similar meaning. The story of Moses being found in an ark of bulrushes in the Nile is definitely derived from the story of the Egyptian Osiris and is a key to the meaning of his life. We learn that Moses was an initiate priest of the Egyptian Mysteries and had received the Rites of Osiris. There is debate as to whether he was a Jew or an Egyptian. In all probability he was neither but had his origin in Asia.

In the spiritual drama Moses plays many parts. Astronomically the sun, he is the symbol of the light-giver and the teacher. In the Eastern esoteric tradition, he is the Manu, Lord of the race, and in all ancient Mystery rituals he appears as the conductor of candidates. In Parsifal he is the old knight Gurnemanz; in the Grail legends of King Arthur, he is Merlin. He is always the preceptor, the same Chiron who was the mentor of Achilles. He is not only the wise man; he is the principle of mind. Mind is the master of bodies—experience ever ready to guide youth—accumulated knowledge always at the disposal of him who would learn.

Infant humanity in its search for truth was never left without leadership. It has recently been stated that Michaelangelo placed horns on his statue of Moses by mistake. In reality however they are most significant. They are the horns of Jupiter Ammon, the same symbol which is later to appear again as the horns on the corners of the Hebrew altar. The horns are those of the celestial Ram, Aries, the leader of the flocks of heaven. The symbol arose from the fact that during the time of Moses, the vernal equinox took place in the sign of the Ram, and the horned Sun was the symbol of truth. Ram, the mind-light god of the Egyptians, is likewise represented as wearing a helmet adorned with the curling horns of rams.

MOSES RECEIVING THE TABLES OF THE LAW

In the racial evolution of man, the patriarchal system was consummated by the Age of Prophets. Among primitive peoples, the old men of the tribes are consulted as oracles. Great teachers, perfect in wisdom, are, so to speak, the old men of humanity, the wise ones, the patriarchs of the race. As the story develops, it further appears that Moses is regarded as synonymous with the occult sciences themselves and the everlasting order of initiate priests who perpetuated them.

To the Egyptians, the Nile was the river of life, the sacred waters which flowed from heaven. These waters later appear in the Christ cycle when the Messiah refers to himself as the living waters which come down from heaven. In the Mosaic cycle, Moses brings the water out of the rock, a definite reference to the release of spiritual knowledge from literal symbols.

It is Moses who led the children of Israel out of Egypt. With them went also Aaron. When Moses desired to go before the Pharaoh he cried to the Lord "I am slow of speech and of slow tongue!" (Exodus 4:10) Therefore the Lord bade him take with him his brother Aaron: When Moses complains that he is slow of speech the reference is definitely to the Mystery Schools, for the secrets of the spirit cannot easily be communicated to men. For this reason, the Egyptian god Harpocrates, keeper of the Mysteries, is depicted with his finger to his lips commanding silence. Aaron is therefore the voice of Moses. He is the priesthood, the custodians of the Mysteries. It is the priest who must clothe the secrets in fables that the foolish may learn something. Pharaoh is the power referred to later by Jesus as "The prince of this world." He is "worldly wisdom" of Bunyan's pilgrim's progress.

Pharaoh is the personification of temporal pomp and splendor, those diversified objects of selfishness, jealousy and greed which keep men in bondage to the least parts of themselves.

The Lord ordered Moses to go unto Pharaoh and when Moses asked by what name God should be known to his children, the Lord said unto him: "I am that I am," (Exodus 3:14). This is one of the most difficult of the Biblical secrets and innumerable interpretations have been given by various sects. In reality it is the only possible definition of First Cause. It reveals the impossibility of bestowing any qualifying or defining terms upon truth or reality. Plato said "God is" and inferred all else that could be said upon that subject as depreciatory. Buddha, when questioned about the ultimate truths of existence, affirmed the Reality of the Real and then remained silent. Socrates taught that to define God was to defile God. This is the true meaning of the "I AM"—truth is what truth is. Even further definition is error.

When Moses went into the court of the Pharaoh, Aaron went with him and, at the command of the Lord, Aaron cast down his rod before Pharaoh and it became a serpent. Likewise did the magicians of Egypt and their rods also became serpents, but the serpent of Aaron swallowed up the little serpents. The magicians of Pharaoh's court, like the scientists of today, represent material knowledge, in itself miraculous and full of wonder, but not in harmony with divine wisdom. The rod of Aaron represents the truth. The serpent form of it is the serpent of wisdom and spiritual truth swallowed up or devoured all the false truth of the material world.

But the Pharaoh, regent of the dark sphere, is not thus easily converted. Like a rich man or a great prince, he clings to his worldly possessions and denies the laws of the universe. As infirmity and misery come to the rich and the powerful, so the plagues descended upon the Pharaoh but he remains adamant until his own son is stricken. In the same way, in a world filled with misery and sorrow, men think little of spiritual matters until their own personal possessions are endangered. The Pharaoh permits his whole land to be laid bare and he does not relent, but when his own is afflicted, he cries in terror for mercy.

So Moses, wisdom, brought about finally the release of his people, and Pharaoh let the people go and the Lord (law) led them through the Red Sea and the wilderness, and Moses took the bones of Joseph with him. The Red Sea is a very apt symbol for man's world of desire. After he overcomes his material nature (the escape from Egypt) he must still conquer his emotions. The way of liberation is through the conquest of desire. And wisdom led the people and the sea opened, and the children of Israel passed through dry shod. Pharaoh, still desiring to destroy evolving humanity, went against the tribes with six hundred chariots, but the sea closed upon them and destroyed them all. Strangely enough, the mummy of the Pharaoh of the Exodus is now preserved in the Cairo Museum. He did not drown in the sea but is believed to have died of the smallpox. Maybe this disease was the Red Sea that engulfed him. Today in civilization a great economic age is drawing to a close. Pharaoh again sends forth his chariots and again a Red Sea may swallow him up—a sea of war and social chaos. Selfishness, pride and greed must always be destroyed by the flame in men themselves, devoured finally by the fire of their own passions.

The children of Israel, humanity, go forth on their wandering, forty years in the desert of waiting. These forty years, has the same symbolical significance as the forty days and forty nights of the Deluge and the forty days of Jesus' fasting in the wilderness. The wilderness is this life where oases of rest and peace are few and hardships many. The search is always for the promised land—Canaan, the place of rest.

In the Biblical mysticism, days and time periods are of great importance. It is written in the 19th chapter of Exodus that it was in the third month after the children of Israel had gone out of Egypt that they came to the wilderness of Sinai. It was from the top of the Mountain of the Law that the Commandments were given unto Moses.

THE TABLES OF THE LAW

The receiving of the Ten Commandments on Mt. Sinai is possibly the most dramatic incident in the Old Testament. It is the subject of numerous commentaries and very profound metaphysical speculations. Most of these are entirely unknown to Bible students. Sinai, though pointed out to travelers in the Holy Land as a single peak in the drear desert, is no mountain of earth but the mountain of the gods, the mysterious hill to the clouded summit of which the wisest of mystics have lifted their eyes. It is the mountain of illumination, the high place of realization. The mountain is symbolical of a state of consciousness, the highest degree of final consciousness to which man can ascend. It is the apex of the triangle of matter, the highest part of the world from the heights of which man's inward perception perceives Reality.

The practice of metaphysical disciplines brings with it the sense of upliftment. The Yogi entering Samadhi feels himself lifted far above the world and its attachments. In one interpretation, we learn that the laws that govern the race come from the highest part of the consciousness of the race itself. No actual hands placed the tablets in the hand of Moses, but the ever-living truth engraved with letters of living power is the laws of the universe upon the two hemispheres of the brain. In the case of Moses as the wise man who leads the race, the Commandments are part of wisdom itself which Moses brings from the height of his own realization down to the valley where mortals dwell who cannot see the light. At this point, the allegory is a supreme accomplishment in fable weaving. Moses descending the mountain perceives that the children of Israel have fallen into sin and are worshipping a golden calf. They are unworthy to receive the ten great truths of life, so Moses breaks the sapphire tablets and substitutes for them two rough-hewn blocks of stone. The enlightened may perceive the preciousness of truth but the multitudes must obey laws of stone.

In the Cabala it is written that Moses three times ascended Sinai, remaining forty days and forty nights upon each occasion. On the first ascent, he was given the tablets which constituted the basis of the TORAH. Upon the second ascent, he received the MISCHNA or the Unwritten Law for the priests. And upon the third ascent he received the CABALA, the soul of the soul of the Law which was given only to the initiates of the Mysteries. It is thus revealed that there are three codes of law—one for the foolish, one for the learned, and one for the illumined. The fable continues that the stone upon which the Law was given was originally formed of heavenly dew and was set in the divine Stone. This stone was broken in half by the breath of God and the figures of the Law were drawn upon the two parts in black fire. The stone was a transparent sapphire and Moses was able to read the letters through the stone. It is this sapphire, the true Secret Doctrine, that Moses refused to reveal to the people. The original tablets did not contain the

Ten Commandments that we know but ten mysterious words, the names of the ten parts of the universe. The sacred decad of the Pythagoreans here appears in the metaphysics of the Jews—ten the perfect number, the basis of the decimal system, the summary of the nine units and the cipher, the mathematical tool by which every secret of nature can be discovered.

The stone tablets which Moses had substituted for the divine gem became an object of adoration, and after the building of the Tabernacle was enshrined in its Holy of Holies. Later it was placed in King Solomon's Temple and finally, like nearly every vestige of truth that appears in this world, the tablets vanished entirely.

THE TABERNACLE IN THE WILDERNESS

The Tabernacle of the Jews was a temple patterned after the great shrines of the Egyptians. The original form and design of the Tabernacle was given by Moses. The children of the twelve tribes supplied the materials and ornamented the Tabernacle from the store of their possessions. This moveable temple is an appropriate symbol of religion itself. Truth is not given unto any one person or in any one place but moves about the earth, entrusted to the noblest and wisest of human beings.

The general form of the Tabernacle is definitely derived from the temples of Karnak and Philae. The Egyptians built in everlasting stone, but nomadic shepherds found the tent more practical than the temple. Josephus gives an excellent description not only of the Tabernacle itself but of its priests, its festivals and its implements. The Cabalistic rites contribute a wealth of lore and mystical interpretation to every part of the Tabernacle and its equipment. The Cabalists agree that the Tabernacle in the Wilderness is a symbol or figure of the universe, a microcosm or miniature representation of the vast sidereal order. These same learned rabbis also insist that the Tabernacle is man himself, not only his physical body but his complete metaphysical constitution. As man is a miniature of the whole world so the Tabernacle is an emblem or similitude of the whole world.

The ancient Greeks taught that the universe was the proper temple and that man worshipping his God should contemplate upon the heavens and the earth. The universe is the living temple of the universal spirit and man's human body is the living temple of his own human spirit. The ancient commentaries declare that the Tabernacle of the Lord is in the Sun and that in man the heart corresponds to the Sun and is the dwelling place of the Most

High.

The Tabernacle in the Wilderness consisted of three parts. First an outer court consisting of a wall of curtains stretched between wooden uprights. Within this wall was an enclosure and in the midst of this enclosure the Tabernacle itself, a tentlike structure divided into two rooms. The larger or outer room was of the proportion of a double cube and the proportion of the inner room was a single cube. The outer room was called the Holy Place and the smaller inner room the Holy of Holies. These three parts of the Tabernacle were symbolic of the three parts of the universe. The outer courtyard represented the elements, the symbols of material or mundane existence. The Holy Place containing the seven-branched candlestick was the sidereal world, the abiding place of the seven planets, the astral sphere. The smaller inner room corresponded to the sphere of the fixed stars, the heavens or constellational diffusion. The cherub figures woven upon the hangings of this inner room represented the star-angels whose patterns filled with eyes are embroidered upon the curtains of heaven.

Paracelsus, the Cabalist, says that man's spirit comes from the stars, his soul from the planets, his body from the elements. This is the arrangement set forth in the structure of the Tabernacle and is an important key to the interpretation of all sacred places, shrines and temples. These three divisions also represent three states of consciousness. The lowest is ignorance, the second is knowledge, and the third is wisdom or illumination. In the Tabernacle rites these three states of consciousness are represented by classes of human beings: ignorance by the multitudes, knowledge by the priests, and wisdom by the high priest who alone could enter the Holy of Holies, for only perfect wisdom may gaze upon the face of the Infinite and live.

The three parts of the Tabernacle correspond therefore to the three revelations made to Moses upon Sinai. The outer court is the Torah or the written law, the Holy Place is the Mischna or soul of the law; and the Holy of Holies is the Cabala, the soul of the soul of the law. The three parts of the Tabernacle appear in nearly all of the ancient Mystery ritual systems. They are the three degrees of the Blue Lodge in Freemasonry; the three degrees of the Egyptian Mysteries of Osiris; and the three parts or dramas of the Eleusinian Rites. One of the first great initiation temples of the world was the Great Pyramid of Gizeh. This structure also contains three rooms, in order of ascent as follows: the pit or subterranean chamber; the Queen's chamber; and the King's chamber. Neophytes seeing the Master of the Secret House passed through elaborate rituals performed in these chambers and their connecting passageways.

The utensils of the Tabernacle are also significant. At the gateway to the outer court sat the Altar of Burnt Offerings to which the unenlightened brought their sacrifices. This altar is symbolical of the literal aspect of the revelation. It is inevitable that ignorance should obey and fulfill the outer semblance of spiritual understanding. Within the court of the Tabernacle sat the Laver of Purification, its sides encrusted with the mirrors of the women of the twelve tribes. Purification is probationship, preparation for acceptance into the rite. Within the Holy Place of the temple itself sat three objects: the table of shewbread, the seven-branched candlestick, and the altar of burnt incense. The twelve loaves of the shewbread, stacked in two heaps of six each, represent the twelve departments of life which receive and bear witness to the twelve zodiacal hierarchies themselves. The seven-branched candlestick represents the planetary bodies, also the seven Elohim, the seven Days of Creation, the seven great laws of life, the seven races, the seven continents, the seven directions of space, and the seven parts of the human soul. The altar of burnt incense which stands at the entrance of the Holy of Holies signifies the breath and the sacred courses of the inner body atmosphere so familiar to students of Raja Yoga. It is also by its location the larynx, the altar of the sacred Word, the incense representing the songs and chanting's of the priests. The tables of the shewbread are placed at the North side of the Tabernacle and the seven-branched candlestick at the South side. This is because in ancient systems of philosophy the North was the abode of the Karmic gods. The candlestick was placed at the South because in the astronomical procedure the ancients taught that the planets never moved Northward.

Certain Hindu schools teach that the five elements are symbolized by parts of the human body as follows: Earth from the feet to the knees; water from the knees to the waist; fire from the waist to the throat; air from the throat to the forehead; and akasha or ether to the crown of the head. The Tabernacle represents the human body in the same way. The altar of burnt offerings represents the earth; the laver of purification the water; the candlesticks and the shew bread are ascribed to fire representing the two extremes of the emotional nature; the altar of burnt incense is the air; and the Shekinah which hovers over the Ark of the Covenant is the akasha or ether.

Beyond the Holy Place, curtained off from the sight of the profane, was the Holy of Holies. In the midst of this stood the Ark of the Covenant, a box made of wood plated with gold. Upon the top of the ark knelt two cherubs facing each other, the tips of their wings meeting over the center of the ark. The space between the cherubs was termed the Mercy Seat. The ark was fitted with rings through which rods could be passed and the sacred chest was lifted onto the shoulders of men to be carried from place to place. Within the ark itself were three sacred objects: the rod of Aaron that budded, the pot of manna that fell in the wilderness, and the tablets of the Law. When the migrations of Israel were finished and the ark finally came to rest in the Holy of Holies of Solomons Temple, the pot of manna and the rod of Aaron had disappeared and only the tablets of the Law remained.

The spiritual triad is repeated in the three sacred objects contained within the ark. Manna represents spirit or truth or wisdom. It is the food which came down from heaven, for truly is it said that "man doth not live by bread only, but by every word that proceedeth out of the mouth of the Lord doth "man live." (Deut. 8:3) In the New Testament, Christ, the personification of wisdom, is made to say: "I am the living bread which came down from heaven: if any man eat of this bread, he shall live forever." (John 6:51). It should be evident to the most conservative Bible student that the manna is not precipitated dew, as some have suggested, or some transcendent form of bread, but, as the Greeks would have said, is the food of the inner man who lives not upon the fruits of the earth but upon the fruits of righteousness.

In the 17th chapter of Numbers is described the budding of Aaron s rod. Verse 8 reads: "And it came to pass, that on the morrow Moses went into the tabernacle of witness: and, behold, the rod of Aaron for the house of Levi was budded, and brought forth buds, and bloomed blossoms, and yielded almonds." The metaphysician will realize the staff of Aaron to be the spine and the blossoms upon it the ganglia and plexuses that are animated or caused to blossom by the disciplines of regeneration. In another form of metaphysics, the blossoming of the rod refers to the regeneration of the emotional nature of which the flower is a peculiar symbol. The same allegory is used by Wagner in the story of Tannhäuser. The repentant monk is not forgiven by the pope but the staff blossoms to prove divine forgiveness.

The manna, the budded staff, and the tablets of the Law thus represent the spiritual, emotional and physical nature of man and the mysteries thereof. The loss of the manna and Aaron's rod reveals that in the end the metaphysical secrets were lost and only the body or physical interpretation of the law remained.

The cherubs upon the mercy seat represent the four fixed signs of the Zodiac, the four elements, and the four lower natures of man—mental, emotional, vital and physical. The fifth element is in the midst of the other four, so the Shekinah, the mysterious light of splendor hovers over the cherubs guarding the mercy seat. In the Cabala Shekinah is equivalent to the Virgin Sophia of the Gnosis; and is also the Virgin, the mother of the Messiah. It is written that the mystery of the Shekinah may not be written. Of course, it is not a pillar or flame by night nor a column of smoke by day. This is merely an allegorical statement. Shekinah is the mystery of the Presence. It is the contact between the higher and the lower. It is the mother of mysteries; it is even the Great Mother of the Ephesians. The Cabalists insist that in the body of man the Shekinah is a subtle essence, the medium through which the spirit acts upon the blood. In the macrocosm, or the universe, the Shekinah is the mysterious field of energy by means of which the solar light acts upon nature. Its location in man is in the ventricular orifices of the brain. It is the nimbus about the head of the saint, the aureole of light, the witness of the Presence.

As the Tabernacle itself was a symbol of universal law, so the robes of the high priest likewise manifested the cosmic plan. The under-garment of the priest was a fine linen robe, identical in meaning with the one-piece white robe of the Nazarenes. Over this was worn a colored garment that came to the knees, embroidered in various colors, usually with a design of pomegranates. Over this was worn a short jacket, the ephod, to which was fastened the breastplate bearing twelve jewels. On the shoulders of the ephod were two onyx stones, and these with other jewels upon his robes made altogether seven, in addition to the twelve in the breastplate. Upon his head the high priest wore a bonnet or helmet divided by a strip going from back to front. Upon the visor of this bonnet were the words: "Holiness unto the Lord." His robe was hung with seventy-two pomegranates and golden bells which represented seventy-two stars, six for each of the zodiacal signs.

The robes of the high priest represent the invisible spiritual bodies of man, the auras, the true garments of glory. The white linen garment is the purified physical body, the long-colored garment the vital body, the ephod the emotional body, the helmet the mental body, the jewels the seven senses, and the twelve jewels of the breastplate the twelve celestial or zodiacal principles which reside in every human soul. The priest therefore represents the manifested glory of the microcosm, the divine man robed with power. It was this high priest, whose garments revealed him to be the perfected initiate, a divine man, alone who could enter the Holy of Holies and converse with the power that hovered over the mercy seat. In simple words, only the adept can perceive universal realities without the veils which obscure them from the eyes of ordinary mortals.

THE DEATH OF MOSES

In the 34th chapter of Deuteronomy is described the death of Moses. In verse 1 it describes how Moses went up "unto the mountain of Nebo." The ancient Phoenician god of learning was Nebo. The word itself means height in the sense of the height of wisdom or of learning. From the top of Mount Nebo Moses saw the Promised Land but he himself was not permitted to enter therein. "So Moses the servant of the Lord died there in the Land of Moab, according to the word of the Lord." According to the commentaries the Lord of Israel himself buried Moses and he hid the grave. "No man knoweth of his sepulcher until this day."

Moses was not permitted to go into the promised land for the reason that Moses represents the personification of the intellectual principle. He is the teacher. But although the mind shall reach the extremities of learning and perceive truth afar off, yet intellect shall never enter truth. This is a truly Oriental teaching. It is Buddhism in the Bible. The promised land represents peace or Nirvana. The broad plains "over against Jericho" and "all the land of Judah, unto the utmost sea"—all this is but a symbol of the Reality at the end of questing, the consummation of the search for truth. The intellect cannot by its very-nature participate in truth, for reality is higher than the mind. The reason may intellectually consider it but never actually experience it. Illumination is the ceasing of the Self in Reality, so Moses the good man is taken unto the hill of Nebo, the highest point of wisdom, and there in the distance perceives the Real. But there, the mind must die and be hidden in the unknown grave, as Kundry falls dead at the feet of the altar of the Grail in the story of Parsifal. And the people of Israel wept for thirty days and then the mourning's for Moses were ended.

Sincerely yours,

Manly P. Hall

NOTICE

Dear Friend: You can make the delivery of your Student Letter more prompt and less expensive if you will be sure to keep us informed of your change of address. We will be most appreciative of your cooperation in this matter. We hope there will be no more delays in getting your copies to you but if there are please be patient with us and we will be sure that you get your entire series in due time. Thank You.

LETTER NO. 5
THE SECRET DOCTRINE IN THE BIBLE

Dear Friend,

SOLOMON AND THE EVERLASTING HOUSE

Those who have carefully studied the Books of the Old Testament realize that the great part of the text is devoted to genealogies and to historical episodes of comparatively little importance. Most of the characters appearing in the Old Testament histories are not preserved in the profane annals of Nations. A comparison between the Bible and other sacred books of the world reveals that most of the Scriptures contain rambling and pointless pseudo histories.

The various commentaries to the Vedas, the most celebrated of the Hindu sacred writings indicate that certain metaphysical truths are concealed under the so-called genealogies. "Every Sunday School pupil has struggled with the "begats." The time expended in memorizing these amounts to little better than waste. If, however, we translate the proper names and interpret the sequences correctly we can discover many interesting things far beyond the ken of the average Sunday School teacher.

The most important commentaries upon the Old Testament are those which have their foundations in the teachings of the Cabala. These commentaries reveal the most profound Jewish scholarship. They are enriched with tradition and a certain instinctive grasp of values peculiar to the people and culture. The old rabbis pondered every symbol and every character of the Scriptures. They extracted a rare and beautiful metaphysical tradition, which, unfortunately, has never found its way into the textbooks of Christendom. This present section is devoted to the interpretation of the account of the building of Solomons Temple given in the First Book of Kings. The story begins with chapter 5 and continues through chapter 9. For the most part it is taught that this is a true historical account of the actual building of a temple fashioned from rock and wood and ornamented with gold and precious stones. If subjected to analysis however, it becomes apparent, as in the case of Noah's Ark, that we are dealing, not with a historical fact, but a symbolical fact. It is difficult to determine with accuracy at this late date the origin of the story of Solomons Temple. It is most probably derived from Egypt as was the Tabernacle in the Wilderness. The architecture generally associated with the Temple is Babylonian and Chaldean. It is probable that several races and cultures contributed to the symbolism.

The story of the building of the Temple is briefly as follows. After the death of his father, David, Solomon became King of the territories of Israel. The dearest of Solomons friends was Hiram, King of Tyre, with whom Solomon engaged in philosophical discourse. Hiram reminded Solomon that David had desired to build a Temple to the Ever-living God. Hiram further offered his assistance in supplying logs and timber and skilled artisans.

It therefore came to pass that in the 480th year, after the children of Israel had come out of the land of Egypt, the building of the Temple commenced. From the dimensions given in 1 Kings, chapter 6, it is evident that Solomon's Temple was of no great size. It was not much larger than the average modern home, and it is difficult to imagine that 70,000 men bore burdens and 80,000 hewed wood in mountains, with 3,3007 overseers all laboring together for seven years to build this comparatively modest structure.

If a cubit be the distance from the end of the finger to the elbow, about eighteen inches, then the length of Solomon's Temple was ninety feet and the breadth of it thirty feet and the height of it forty-five feet.

Something seems to be wrong in this picture. Various methods of determining the Jewish cubit have been attempted, but in all probability the dimensions we have given are approximately correct. There might be a difference of a few feet.

Of course, there were approaches to the Temple, houses for the priests, chambers for storing sacred utensils, etc., but still there was a wide discrepancy between truth and popular opinion.

The Temple was built on Mt. Moriah, one of the low hills in the cluster upon which the city of Jerusalem is built. There is still a flat rock called the Rock Moriah Jutting from the top of this hill. Today a Mohammedan Mosque occupies the site of Solomon's Temple, and nothing remains of the original edifice except a few mutilated stone carvings which may or may not be genuine.

Solomon and the Everlasting House

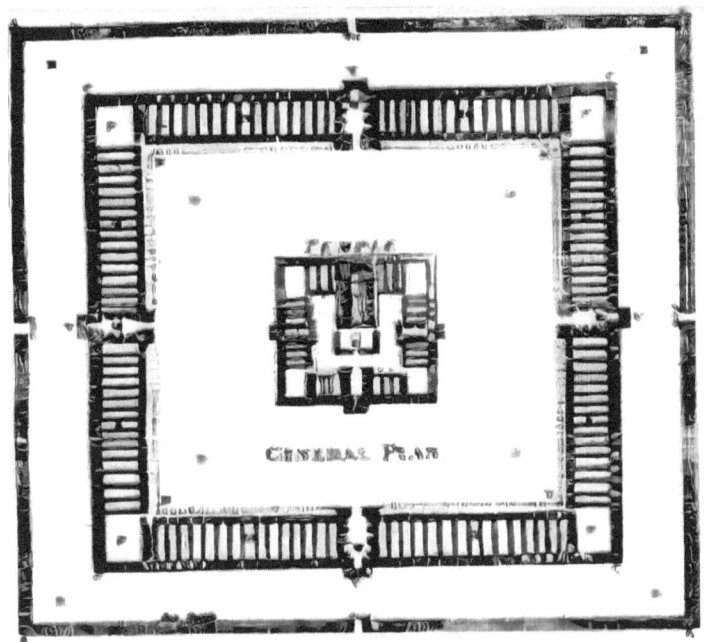

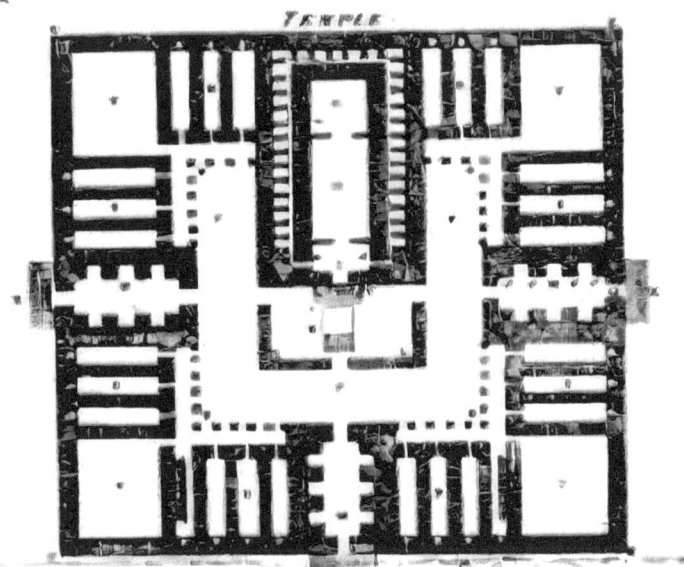

SOLOMON'S TEMPLE

THE UPPER FIGURE SHOWS THE TEMPLE WITH THE COURTYARDS. THE LOWER FIGURE SHOWS THE TEMPLE PROPER WITH THE PORCH IN FRONT, THE INNER COURTYARD, AND C THE HOLY OF HOLIES.

Solomon went to his friend, the King of Tyre, and asked that a clever workman be dispatched to superintend the casting of the vessels of the Temple. In 1 Kings, 7:13, it says: : "that a cunning workman by the name of Hiram was sent out of Tyre" and then verse 14: "he was a widow's son of the tribe of Naphtali and his father was a man of Tyre, a worker of brass; and he was filled with wisdom, and understanding; and cunning to work all works in brass, and he came to King Solomon, and wrought all his work."

Da Costa, in his Dionysian Artificers, declared that Hiram of Tyre was an initiate priest of the Mysteries of Dionysius, one of the initiated order of architects that flourished in the ancient world, and continued down to the Architectural Collegium at Rome. This intimated by the Bible statement that he was a man of wisdom and understanding and a cunning worker in metals, that is, he was an initiate of the mysteries of fire, the only element that will work metals. The story of Hiram, called "Our Father Hiram" or "Hiram Abiff," is the principal theme of the third degree of Blue Lodge Freemasonry. In fact, Freemasonry traces its original symbology to the three Grand Masters of the Lodge of Jerusalem, that is, Solomon, Hiram of Tyre and Hiram Abiff.

When we say that an account in the Bible may have a symbolical meaning it does not necessarily mean that the account is entirely unhistorical. This is evident in the masonic legend of Hiram Abiff. That a cunning workman by the name of Hiram may have lived is not necessarily unreasonable, but it is certain that legends have been built up about the character which belong definitely in the classification of symbolism.

Throughout the Bible we may find mythology and history, fact and fable, closely entwined. Certain apocryphal legends spring up around any outstanding personality. In fact, the legend may come in time to be more important than the man, when the ages have gently shrouded the truth in forgetfulness and obscurity.

When we learn that it required seven years to build Solomon's Temple, we know we have discovered a key to the mystery. Seven is the most sacred of the numbers, associated of course with creative processes, with cosmogony and psychogenesis. In the 7th verse, 1st Kings, chapter 6, it is written "there was neither hammer nor axe nor any tool of iron had in the house, while it was in building." This was indeed a temple "built without sound of hammer or voice of workmen." In fact, this was the Everlasting Temple Eternal in the Heavens. Josephus, the Jewish historian, was aware of the fact that the Tabernacle in the Wilderness was a symbol of the Universe. This is also true of Solomons Temple in even more perfect measure.

The name of Solomon may be divided into three syllables. Sol-Om-On. Each of these syllables is the name of a Sun God or a Divine Principle. Sol means Sun, Om is the sacred syllable of the Vedas, the most magical of all intonations among the Hindus, and On, is the name of a Supreme Being in Persia. The building of the Temple was supervised by three men. Solomon of the Sun, the source of all life and power, Hiram of Tyre, the earth, who supplied the materials, and a cunning workman, Hiram Abiff, the energies of space, the ethers, the dancing power of Fohat, the law of the atoms. The three Grand Masters therefore symbolized the three powers which created the world. It requires seven years to build the Temple, that is, seven periods or cycles are necessary to perfect the earth. The thousands of workers are the forces, energies and atoms. The masters of the workmen are the laws of life, and the finished Temple, so symbolically small, represents the physical Universe itself, comparatively insignificant, but requiring for its creation and preservation the benevolent conspiracies of the innumerable Forces that work in Space.

The Creative Triad here represented by the three Grand Masters is present in all the major theological systems of the world. The Trimurti in the Caves of Elephanta in the harbor of Bombay depicts the principal God of the Hindus with three faces. These faces represent the creative, preservative and disintegrative powers resident in Divine Energy. The three faces of Shiva, as the Trimurti is called in India, symbolizes the Triform creative principle of life. All energy manifests through triads. These triads finally accomplish the building of the soul temple, that is, through the interaction of creative agencies life is gradually matured, brought to ripening. The ultimate perfection toward which all life is inevitably moving may be said to be the work accomplished by the three builders.

The building of Solomon's Temple takes place on several planes simultaneously. The Solar System is a product of creative energies. Each of the planets is a house built in Space. All the races and lives evolving upon the planets are likewise little temples built to manifest the Will of the gods. All forms are houses of the Soul. One Spiritual Principle is building all these houses, functioning through them, finally discarding them for other better houses and forever growing. The realization of this is a mood rather than an intellectual accomplishment. Man is the Master Builder. Each man is building the temple of his own character, he is building the body through which he must function. He is ennobling his emotions, refining his appetites and improving his mind. Those who accomplish greatly in these endeavors are indeed Master Builders. They are building, not houses of wood and stone, but temples fashioned without the sound of hammer or the voice of workmen.

The whole motion of the Universe is toward Truth. Truth is growing up in everything, manifesting through all forms and natures. Truth, therefore, may be called the hidden good, the secret God who dwells in the temples that are built for It according to the law. In the story of Solomon's Temple, we learn that the Holy Place and the most Holy of Holy Places were sanctified to the service of the Living God. The Holy Place of man is his mind and the most Holy of Holy Places is the heart. It is in the heart that the sacrament to consecration must take place; it is in the small room that the whole temple is consecrated; it is in the heart of man that his life is made new.

The Dionysian Artificers concealed under the symbolism of architecture the secret and spiritual mysteries of the regeneration of man. They were truly divine architects, they were building, not houses, but adepts. It says in 1st Kings that the cedars of Lebanon were cut down and were floated to Joppa to become the beams and the uprights of the Everlasting House. The cedars of Lebanon were not trees. There was a Holy Temple upon Mt. Lebanon. As in the case of the Druids, whose name means the "men of the oak trees" the initiates of Mt. Lebanon were called trees or cedars. It was the wisdom of these men that supported the Temple, their knowledge was the beam and wisdom the upright. Houses that endure are not built by man, for their substance is of this earth, but with the secret substances of Wisdom and Knowledge that shall endure all vicissitudes of physical existence.

SONG OF SOLOMON

There is no part of the Old Testament more difficult to interpret than the Song of Songs, which is Solomon. The modern clergy evade this issue and there has been considerable controversy as to the justification of this Book being included among the Scriptures. In truth there is no work more deeply mystical, more profoundly symbolic.

It is generally believed that the Song of Solomon was written about one thousand years before the beginning of the Christian Era. Its terms, its symbols, and its figures are strange to the modern world, but for the lover of deep and hidden lore this brief book is incalculably rich.

The Alchemists of the Middle Ages declared that the Song of Solomon contained the whole secret of the manufacture of artificial gold. Its 8 chapters represented the steps in the purification, calcination and projection of the Philosopher's Stone. We know that the alchemists were really mystical philosophers, but concealed their metaphysics from a cruel and unbelieving world. Gold means soul power, the Philosopher's Stone is Wisdom, therefore the secret of Wisdom and of the perfection of soul must be concealed in that Book which was anciently called the Canticles.

In a very curious and ancient manuscript relating to the transmutation of metals and other alchemistic and mystical processes the base metal which is going to be transmuted into a spiritual stone is described in Solomon 1:5. In the old symbols the black earth or rebus is always represented as a dark untinctured mass. The two principles involved in the perfection of the stone, that is, the dual forces which are to accomplish the purification of the elements are described in chapter 2:1. The sublimation begins in chapter 2:4, the alchemical fires by which the elements are to be tested, chapter 2:7 and chapter 4:16. The putrefaction of death before the resurrection of the elements is described in chapter 3:1, the sublimation or distillation of the universal elixir in chapter 3:6, the coagulation and change of color chapter 6:9 to 14 inclusive. This tells the colors the elements pass through in the making of a stone. The fixation of the crystallization of the stone is described in 2:12 and 8:4. The multiplication of the elements is described in 6:1, the augmentation and final projection of the stone is explained in chapter 8:8 and through to the end of the chapter. This means that in the work is a formula cleverly concealed, meaningless to the uninitiated but of great moment to the informed.

It is believed that the 1st verse of the 2nd chapter of the Song of Solomon— "I am the rose of Sharon, and the lily of the valleys" is the origin of the Rosicrucian symbolism of the rose and lily. This verse appears upon many alchemical plates and symbols, but is never interpreted for the profane. The rose and the lily are the symbols of love and wisdom and these must be well understood before the molten sea of the adept can be cast.

In the Song of Solomon there are two characters, Solomon, the king, and a mysterious dark Princess. We have already explained the meaning of Solomon, how this king symbolizes the Sovereign Intelligence of the world. He was the wisest of all kings and his wisdom endured forever. He is the personification of Divine Power and Divine Authority.

The black Princess reminds us of the black star, the black Diana of Ephesus, the black Mylitta, the black Virgin of early European Christianity. She is the hidden Mother, the black Isis, Sophia, Mother of Mysteries. In substance she is the Mother of the Gods to whom Julian, the Emperor, addressed his hymns of praise. The dark Mother is called by the Greeks the womb of night, the darkness in the midst of which shines the light power, Solomon in all his glory. The Song of Songs, therefore, is the story of creation. It is a mystical description of the Sun and the earth, for the earth is indeed the dark Mother, Coatlicue, the dark Earth Mother of the Aztecs.

The masters of the Cabala examined deeply into the story of Solomon and the dark Earth Mother. Their findings were in substance as follows: all things manifest themselves from a mysterious obscurity, the origin of life is concealed, the end of life is concealed. The visible world is rounded with the darkness, with origins and ultimates hidden from mortal perception. The Egyptians termed the mysterious veil which hides the superphysical from the physical the "Veil of Isis." The Alexandrian hermetists called this veil the thrice deep darkness, for in it are concealed three things, the mystery of life, the mystery of thought and the mystery of feeling. The Babylonians made Ishtar their principal goddess, the daughter of Sin, the God of the Moon, the lighter of the night. All this symbolism teaches us that we are to understand an ancient philosophy to the effect that the true source of all things is called the mother or matrix. From this darkness emerge all living things, progeny of night, so Hesiod calls night the Mother of the Gods. This night or darkness is infinitely related to light. Day and night follow themselves, the eternal alternation. Day is Solomon, night is the Dark Goddess.

There is a fine Hindu fable to illustrate this. Shiva, the Sun, falls in love with Parvati, the daughter of Himalaya, the God of the mountains. The Sun God, Shiva, comes to court Parvati when he meets the mountains of the western sky at sunset. For a moment he rides upon the mountain tops, for the great bull, Nandi, is the earth. From the union of Shiva, the Sun, and Parvati, the sunset, is born Kali, the Goddess of night, worshiped throughout India as the black daughter of the Sun. Thus, we see that the black Goddess represents not destruction or evil, but merely the dark origin of things. We find this again in the Gnostic systems where the Virgin Sophia or Wisdom becomes the heroine of strange and curious fables. It was from the Gnostics that the troubadours or wandering musicians of the Middle Ages had their origin. The troubadours were the sweet singers of songs and they always sang of a mystical and unknown woman, the Virgin of the world. These sonnets soon came to be regarded as merely love songs, but in their origin, they were mystical hymns of adoration to the Mother of the world. Dante and Beatrice, the dark woman of Shakespeare's sonnets, are both statements of the same myth, rooted in history, but not significant as history.

The spirit of man is regarded as a luminous principle perfect in wisdom, the origin of the life in man. This spirit, descending into dark bodies, achieves through the chemistry of experience the mysterious power that is called Soul. The Virgin of the world is Soul, in the Universe the World Soul, in man the human soul. The soul is the dark Princess. This we find clearly stated in the Book of Revelation, where Jerusalem, adorned as a bride, comes down out of heaven adorned for her husband, chapter 21:2. The dark Princess is the bride of the Lamb. It is the soul born out of the body, possessing within itself no light, but reflecting the light of the spirit.

Let us think then in these terms. Man, having perfected his material evolution, and having reached that condition of spiritual development in which he becomes aware of his own divine nature, yearns to be united forever with the spiritual truth and reality that are the very substance of himself. The great Sri Ramakrishna taught that the truth of all things was the Great Mother. He thought of God in terms of the mother of all life. When he ended his meditation, he passed into a state of ecstasies. He wrote many books describing his understanding of spiritual reality. His words are not so different from those contained in the Song of Songs, soul crying for the real, the spiritual self-reaching down to embrace its lower nature and lift it up into one with itself. This is the mystery of the Song of Songs. The old rabbins knew the secret of the lifting up of self. They realized that this secret had been strangely but beautifully concealed in the Song of Solomon.

PROVERBS

The Book of Proverbs is attributed to Solomon and should be understood as reflecting the wisdom and culture of Israel at that time. The difficulty we have today is the lamentably bad translations of these scriptural books. All the subtility of the originals vanished centuries ago leaving a mass of material still interesting but lacking a certain vitality. We may use one example to summarize the entire situation. In chapter 1:7, it reads "the fear of the Lord is the beginning of knowledge." Now, technically and philosophically speaking, this is untrue, for we are taught to love the Lord, our God, and love and fear cannot abide together, so we wonder what might originally have been intended. By examining the oldest traditions available we learn that this verse says that the Sod is for the Chasidim. Now the word Sod has been translated 'fear of the Lord' but the actual word has no such meaning. Sod means an assemblage. It may mean technically a group of initiated priests and by rational extension the doctrines or teachings of such a group in its larger sense, therefore Sod means the wisdom of the initiate or the esoteric doctrine, but this does not mean the fear of the Lord. Now the Chasidim were priests who had been accepted as disciples or initiates into all of the ancient mysteries. This is a restatement of another verse in the scriptures which says "The wisdom of God is for those who fear him." These two verses have identical meanings. Let us therefore say for Proverbs 1:7 the esoteric doctrine is the beginning of wisdom or the esoteric doctrine is for those who have been accepted into the mysteries. These are indeed the "true sayings" referred to in verse 6, the hidden teachings. But what does this mean to the average Bible student. This enthusiastic jot and tittle worshiper will insist that the words of the King James version are the very words of God Himself. The beginning of blasphemy is to doubt the wisdom of that decrepit group of old men who made the translation. Time and time again you run against these mistakes and every statement contained in the Bible should be checked with the Greek or Hebrew originals before any interpretation is derived therefrom.

It does not necessarily follow that all of the translations are incorrect. A considerable part of Proverbs is devoted to moral teaching with special emphasis upon the desirability of wisdom. Solomon, the son of David, exhorts those who would be close to God to achieve wisdom. Of course, in his day there were not great schools and libraries available to the people. To him wisdom was the accumulated knowledge of his tribe, the law and tradition handed down from father to son, see chapter 1:8. Thus the Book of Proverbs is in strange contradiction to the most familiar teachings of modern Christianity. Solomon cries out that man must be wise. He invites those who love truth to incline their ears unto wisdom and apply their hearts to understanding. Yet in the New Testament the emphasis is entirely upon faith. Solomon says of wisdom that "she is more precious than rubies; and all the things thou canst desire are not to be compared unto her" Chapter 3:15. Solomon also teaches that wisdom is found in ways of godliness. Only the man who seeks God can partake of wisdom. How different this is from our modern viewpoint.

The modern scientist has rejected the inferences of religion. Atheism and agnosticism are rampant in the world. Men believe they can be wise without being good, but this can never happen, for wisdom and virtue are inseparably related. If modern thinkers would realize that deepness of understanding requires a spiritual perspective we would have less of war and struggle and conflict and more of the peace and security which are described in the Book of Proverbs.

What is wisdom? Wisdom is knowledge perfected through inward realization. Wisdom comes not out of books nor does truth come out of books. Understanding and wisdom come from within man, they sanctify knowledge, they transmute and perfect education, they spiritualize thought and culture.

Why was Plato a wise man while some modern thinker is only educated? The modern man may possess far more actual technical knowledge, he may not suffer from Aristotle's inability to number correctly the teeth in the human head; yet the man who can number the teeth and split the atoms may be an ignorant man, while some Indian sage seated under a banyan tree, with none of this world's goods and no schooling, may be a truly great man. If education could bestow wisdom, we would all be wise, but instead of this we are foolish, filled with prejudices and conceits, incapable of even friendliness and honesty.

It is therefore appropriate to meditate upon wisdom even as Solomon meditated upon it. Wisdom is the most precious thing in the world. It bestows absolute security; it makes man one with the SOVEREIGN TRUTH which sustains the Universe. Plato was wise because he transmuted knowledge into soul power. This great man, gentle and patient, too wise to be angry, too learned to be unjust, is a magnificent example of the breadth and depth the true wisdom bestows. A comparison between a modern scientist and Plato would be most humiliating for the modern scientist. He may know more but he understands so little of what he knows. He has convinced himself that there is neither God nor reason in the Universe, therefore there is no truth, no wisdom within himself. Plato saw God in everything and communed with truth. The modern scientist sees God in nothing and may commune only with his confreres obsessed with similar unbelief.

Solomon tells us something else in the Proverbs. He tells us that it is impossible to be wise without living in harmony with the Divine Plan. Only the soul that is gentle and filled with the love of truth is capable of great learning, and no man can learn more than he himself is. Increase of knowledge infers increase of spiritual stature. As we grow in integrity, we become capable of greater knowledge.

In another place Proverbs 9:1, Solomon writes "wisdom hath builded her house, she hath hewn out her seven pillars" and what are the seven pillars of wisdom? They are the seven laws which sustain the Universe, they are the seven aspects of the real. It is true that wisdom hath builded her house and her house is the Universe, and has not that Power which builded it the wisdom to sustain it. Man, immersed in wisdom, is still foolish. Surrounded everywhere by the evidences of truth he is still ignorant and perverse. In the presence of the Mystery of Life he lives not at all.

Proverbs also tells us that the wicked man cannot flourish. Chapter 11:5 reads "the righteousness of the perfect shall direct his way; but the wicked shall fall by his own wickedness." The whole world desires to be happy, it desires security and peace, it longs for green pastures, but happiness must be earned. The stupid, the foolish and the selfish can never be happy. Any man who departs from wisdom departs from peace. A man who clings to the evils in him must suffer for his decision. It appears in this world that the evils flourish, but if we examine closely into their lives we shall see sorrow, misery, sickness and death. The law forbids that any man who is not intrinsically good shall enjoy either wisdom or peace.

Although the Proverbs are attributed to Solomon, no man knows for certain by whom they were written, but whoever he was, the author of these verses was indeed a wise man. He was a Master of the Mysteries of Life, an adept of secret schools. In 12:28 he says "in the way of righteousness is life; and in the pathway thereof there is no death." This is indeed the teaching of the mysteries of the sacred temples of Eleusis and Sais. Immortality is the reward of wisdom, not immortality in the sense of the perpetuation of the physical body with its infirmities, but rather a conscious participation in eternal life. The wise man perceives the law, obeys it, and his inner life is perfected.

Our modern dictators might profit by the verse "better it is to be of a humble spirit with the lowly, than to divide the spoil with the proud." Man lives a little time in this world and departs into the unknown from whence he came. This life is indeed an antechamber of eternity. How little we appreciate the impermanence of our physical existence, how seldom we look beyond this life. Perceiving only this physical existence we live wholly for the day, ignoring and refusing to consider our eternal existence, but time brings to all things the rewards of action. Each person in the end comes to that which is his own. We may regret the seeming injustice of life, but there is a mighty honesty in Space and all men and their deeds shall finally come to their just deserts.

The student of the Christian Bible will do very well to consider the sacred books of other Nations. It is also important for the Biblical student to have the religious literature of the world ever available to him. He soon realizes from the study of comparative religion that the Scriptures of various peoples have a common origin and a common purpose. Not one of the Scriptural Books is complete in itself. Each is derived from the writings and customs of several racial doctrines.

Religious intolerance must be overcome by all sincere truth seekers. The age of bigotry has passed. Evolving humanity demands and deserves a more tolerant religious perspective. We like to feel that sincere students have outgrown an intolerant addiction to any sect or creed. On the other hand, it is impossible for mam to function normally without some spiritual guidance. Our present international chaos is due to the failure of idealism in the affairs of men. This failure is due, at least in part, to religion itself, that is, what we call religion. It is due to the intolerance of sects and innumerable superstitions that have been foisted upon a gullible humanity. The commercialism of religion is greatly to be deplored but is inevitable under existing world conditions.

To the average Christian the Old Testament is a book of history, bad and garbled, a history ridden with intolerance and cruelty, but so are the Vedas of India, the Koran of Mohammed, the Zend-Avesta of the Persians. The greatest of the Indian classics, the Bhagavad Gita, is the story of a war, a war of brothers. Krishna comes to Arjuna on the battlefield of Kurukshetra. The wars of Scripture, the massacres and the captivities, are all symbolical. They all represent the great battle of life itself. In the Nordic myths we have the battle between the gods and demons on the planes of Asgard that ended finally in the destruction of the world.

It seems incredible to an intelligent person that any sane man or woman could have accepted literally the spiritual significance of the Old Testament's war and carnage, yet millions of people today live by the jot and tittle of such literalism. This the sincere student must definitely avoid. He must search for the divine mystery in all things, and discovering the true keys to the Scriptures, must apply them, not only to the Book but to the mystical art of living itself.

Yours sincerely,

Manly P. Hall

LETTER NO. 6
THE SECRET DOCTRINE IN THE BIBLE

Dear Friend,

In connection with the previous letter, it is interesting to identify the Queen of Sheba according to the cabalistic system. The word Sheba means seven. She is, therefore, the queen of the seven and represents the spinal fire in the human body. She is Kundauni, the serpent goddess of the seven chakras. The Queen of Sheba comes from Ethiopia, or the Land of Darkness. She journeys to Jerusalem bearing rich treasures for the Everlasting House. In occult anatomy, the Land of Darkness is at the base of the spine. It is from here that coiled kundalini rises slowly to the brain, awakening the chakras. This ascent is frequently referred to as a journey. In the Bible, it is a visit to Jerusalem, which means not only the City of Peace, but also the city of stacks or heaps, an arcane reference to the convolutions of the brain.

THE GREAT MAN OF NEBUCHADNEZZAR'S DREAM

In the second chapter of the Book of Daniel, beginning at verse 21 and continuing through verse 45, is the account of a strange dream that came to the King of Babylon. The King beheld a great image, the head of which was of fine gold, its shoulders and arms of silver, its body of brass, its legs of iron, and its feet a mixture of iron and clay. As the great figure stood in all its glory, a cubic stone was mysteriously cut from a quarry and cast by invisible hands at the feet of the great image. As the stone struck the feet, the image was destroyed, changing into fine dust. The cube afterward grew greater in size until it became as vast as a mountain.

The explanation given by Daniel is definitely misleading. The prophet explains to Nebuchadnezzar that the golden head, the silver arms and shoulders, the brazen body, the iron legs, and the feet of iron and clay symbolize empires that shall fall one after the other. From this conceit has arisen much confusion in modern theology. Every nation of the ancient and modern world has been associated with the parts of Nebuchadnezzar's image. The second Adventists have rejoiced at, and various Bible societies have announced the millennium as a result of calculations based upon the parts of this symbolic figure. These millennianites have been fixing dates for the "second coming" for nearly a thousand years, "but the end is not yet." This is a fair example of the general lack of research and scholarship evident among most groups of religious enthusiasts.

The figure of Nebuchadnezzar's dream is definitely a macrocosmic man, the great cabalistic man of the Zohar, the Adam Kadmon, the world symbol later revived in Alexandria under the name Serapis. The Alexandrian Serapis, as described by the early church fathers, was a figure composed of many metals and substances, including even plants. It was worshipped as an epitome of nature, divine and human. Therefore, its upper parts were of more precious substances, and its lower pans of baser materials.

Although the description given in Daniel is somewhat mutilated, nevertheless the symbolism is apparent. The head of the image is of gold, the upper body and arms of silver, the lower body of bronze, and the legs and feet of a substance composed of the mingling's of iron and clay. Compare these with the four ages of the Greeks, the gold, the silver, the bronze, and the iron; also, with the four yugas of the Hindus, of which the lowest or fourth, the kali yuga, corresponds closely with the feet of iron and clay.

The ancient Zohar says that the four worlds were represented by four Adams, or the four parts of one colossal figure "whose body nature is, and God the soul." This great figure is always described by the cabalists with its face in profile without eyelids, and ornamented with a long beard ending in thirteen points. The head of this being is gold, symbolizing the pure nature of divinity, the head of all life. The silver arms and shoulders correspond to the active parts, the hierarchies, which emanate from the golden head. They are the builders, the angels, the archangels, the seraphim and the cherubim, the thrones and the dominations, and the principalities. The bronze body is the zodiac, the planets, the material cosmos, the forms of the hierarchies above. And, lastly, the fourth world of iron and clay represents the earth, which, according to the ancient philosophers, was girded by a wall of iron. Here the iron is the firmament and the clay the planet earth itself.

Nor do the analogies end here, for the figure represents the cycles of generation. The head is birth, the shoulders growth, the body maturity, the legs age, and the feet death. Here also is represented the constitution of man: the mental body gold, the emotional body silver, the vital body bronze, and the higher and lower parts of the physical body iron and clay. The figure, therefore, is a kind of sephiroth, a tree in the form of a man, a tree that bears the world and the heavens upon its branches and represents in its various parts the divisions of both the macrocosm and the microcosm. Here, also, is signified the five races and the four world periods, the fourth being divided into two parts, the Mars-Mercury halves of the earth period.

The cubic stone in the Christian Cabala has been exoterically interpreted as Christ. This is the stone the builders rejected, but which becomes the head of the corner. The theologians would have us believe that the ages and the law, the cycles and the worlds, the mechanism of the ancient Mysteries were all dissolved and destroyed by the Messianic dispensation. But consider the symbolism of the cube. It is the most perfect of the geometric solids, being equal in all its parts. It consists of six faces which represent the days of creation, and of twelve lines which symbolize the zodiac. If each of the faces be open to the core, the result will be a cruciform design consisting of six pyramids. Each of the separate pyramids will have four faces, which total twenty-four, the number of the elders before the throne in Revelation, and also the hours of the day. If the twenty-four be added to the six faces of the cube, the result will be thirty, the degrees of a zodiacal sign, and a twelfth part of a circle. It is written, therefore, that the perfect cube is symbolic of the New Jerusalem, the "city foursquare."

According to the Pythagoreans, the cube is a symbol of both matter and man, the opening of the cube being a symbol of the unfoldment of man and the releasing of geometric mysteries within himself. To the Christian, Christ is the perfect man; therefore, he becomes the embodiment of the perfect measure of a man, the cube. In Freemasonry, the perfect ashlar or trued stone is the proper figure of the perfect man, for he is square, upright, and true, which are the moral qualities of a cube. The perfect cube represents the personality that has had all the unevenness, roughness, and inequality polished away by experience. Such a stone is ready to become a block, in the Everlasting House not built by hands but eternal in the heavens.

If, then, Nebuchadnezzar's man symbolizes the universe and the world, and the stone symbolizes the adept, the perfect man, then we understand how worldliness is dissipated by wisdom, how the material universe is overcome by that which is square and true, and being overcome is entirely dissipated, leaving "not a rack behind." We now understand why this cube stone becomes larger and larger until it becomes a mountain. Wisdom itself is frequently symbolized by a mountain or hill. Truth, having overcome error, fills the whole world with itself, increasing greatly in size. It fills the life of him to whom it is revealed.

THE STORY OF SAMSON

The life of Samson is given in Judges 13-16, inclusive. Careful study will show that the entire account is a cleverly concealed myth which parallels very closely the Greek myth of Hercules. The name Hercules means the glory of Hera (who was the Queen of Heaven). In Hebrew, Samson means sunlike. Samson is a solar personification, and, like Hercules, performs certain labors consistent with his role. The myth was devised evidently when the vernal equinox occurred in Taurus, or at least under the influence of such a concept. It is especially interesting to note that the strength of Samson lay in his seven locks of hair. In classical symbolism, the hair of the sun-god represents his rays or powers. For this reason, the infant sun-god, born at the winter solstice, is represented with one lock of hair. Its powers, or rays, increase as it moves from the winter solstice to the summer solstice. Under these conditions, it will reach the summer solstice in Leo with seven locks of hair.

One of the great labors of Hercules was the slaying of the Nemean lion and dressing in its skin. Samson likewise slew a lion and found honey in the carcass. The sun, reaching Leo, is robed in the sign of the celestial lion, its essential dignity according to astrology. By the same rule, the carrying away of the gates of Gaza would correspond with the vernal equinox when the sun breaks away from the captivity of winter.

The sign of Leo is followed by Virgo, the virgin, which is Delilah. This is the sun's first sign of decreasing light. Delilah, therefore, after three unsuccessful attempts, discovers the secret of his strength, and, at the autumnal equinox, cuts off his hair or rays. Later he is blinded, further to emphasize his loss of power. But finally in death, the winter solstice, he destroys the house of the Philistines by bringing down the two central columns.

This is a grand astronomical myth, and has a certain Messianic significance. It should be remembered that all sun-gods are prototypes of the Christ, or phases of the Christ mythos. An early theological writing says that Christ by his death destroyed death and brought an end to evil in the world. This is perfectly prefigured by Samson tearing down the house of the Philistines and dying himself to destroy the wicked. As Samson's seven locks of hair were the secret of his strength, so the Lamb of God bled from seven wounds.

All sun-god myths are indicative not only of the sun in the sky, but the small sun or spirit in man which achieves emancipation by the performance of the twelve labors which make his zodiac of experience. Thus, all of the world saviors are personifications of humanity's struggle for truth and final accomplishment of immortality.

THE VISION OF EZEKIEL

THE VISION OF EZEKIEL

The opening chapters of the book of Ezekiel are devoted to a mysterious vision that occurred while the prophet was among the captives by the river of Chebar. The metaphysical experiences described in the Bible most frequently occur near water. In religious symbolism, water is a symbol of the etheric world that extends beyond the physical plane of life. The river Styx across which Charon rows the dead symbolizes the etheric interval between the physical and astral planes. Of similar significance is the river Jordan upon whose farther shore await the souls of the redeemed according to Christian religious enthusiasts. The Nile was sacred to Egypt, and the pious Brahmin hopes to die beside the Ganges. Rivers are universally significant of transition.

Thus, it occurs that Ezekiel receives his strange vision on the shores of the etheric consciousness. The river Chebar is that mystic stream which flows between the material and divine worlds. The account therefore, very definitely is indicative that the prophet Ezekiel received his vision while in a state between physical and superphysical consciousness. The occultist knows that it is ever thus that visions come.

Ezekiel beheld a whirlwind coming out of the north, a great cloud filled with fire, in the midst of which appeared the chariot of the Most High. The direction from which the vision came is of the greatest importance. In the teachings of the Egyptians, the north was regarded as the abode of the gods. In one secret metaphysical system, it is clearly set forth that a temple of the gods must have an eastern, a southern, and a western gate, but at the north there shall be no gate. The ancients devised this belief because to them the sun never appeared in the northern part of the heavens. The Egyptians' polar mountain was the abode of the old, dark gods, the fathers of the divine kings. The mysterious Meru of the Hindus, the mountain of the gods, is a polar mountain, as, likewise, Shamballa whose ridgepole is the polar axis. As the gods dwelt in the north, men might not travel there. In honor of the gods, the northern part of the temple was without gate or opening, to signify the unapproachable majesty of divinity and the secret abode of the most holy spirits. Hence, it was from the north, from the axis mountain that the whirling vision of Ezekiel came. This indicates beyond any doubt that the prophet Ezekiel was wise in the learning of the Egyptians and had accepted their concepts of the northern mysteries.

Out of the whirlwind from the north, there appeared an extraordinary instrument of power. The Bible gives no name to the chariot of majesty, but by the Hebrews it is called the Mercavah. The Mercavah was so sacred to the old rabbins that it might be spoken of only with the greatest veneration and only in the presence of the elders and among the elders. The Mercavah is one of the deepest mysteries of cabalism.

The chariot of righteousness, the seat of the Most High, the mystery of the wheels that go all ways and are filled with eyes, is thus interpreted by the wisest of the cabalists: The chariot consists of four creatures called cherubs, each going a different way, each with four heads, six wings, and the hoofs of a calf. Each of the cherubs bore the face of a man, a bull, a lion, and an eagle, and their wings met at the corners of the Mercavah. These mysterious creatures rode on wheels filled with eyes, and above them was a throne chair, and upon the throne was an awful presence in white, surrounded by light and power and accompanied by a rainbow. So numerous and complicated are the interpretations of this vision that we can mention only a small part of them.

In simple statement, the Mercavah is the world or universe as the body or vehicle of the Creator. It is beneath his feet, for the earth is his footstool. The Mercavah is the footstool wherein God is manifest only in his lesser parts. We, therefore, shall discover an astronomical significance in the form and structure of the Mercavah. The cherubs are the symbols of the four cardinal angles, the equinoxes and the solstices. It must be remembered that at the time this vision was described, the equinoxes fell in Taurus and Scorpio, and the solstices in Aquarius and Leo. These four signs are the bull, the eagle, the man, and the lion, respectively. These four signs not only occur frequently in the ancient Jewish metaphysics, and the occult sciences of the Greeks and Egyptians, but reappear in the Christian mysteries in the forms of the symbols attributed to the four evangelists who, as St. Augustine observed, were witnesses unto the four corners of the world. The sarcophagi of princes and prelates are frequently adorned with the four creatures, and they reoccur consistently in religious architecture.

The cherubim or living creatures are the four great guardians of the four corners of the sky or earth. We find them even in the mythology of the American Indians. Ancient astronomers on the plains of Chaldea established four great stars which appeared in the four constellations, Aquarius, Leo, Taurus, and Scorpio, calling them the guardian angels. Each of the four guardians had six wings, which together make the 24 hours of the day. They also represented the zodiacal galaxies of stars, for it is written in the cabalistic books that the stars are the eyes of the angels, and that the bodies of the angels are full of eyes. In the Apocalypse occur the four horsemen who are an aspect of the same symbolism. And among the North American Indians, there were giant chieftains guarding the homes of the four winds.

In the Greek theology, Phanes burst from the egg of chaos ornamented with the heads of birds and animals, and almost identical in description with the cherubim of Ezekiel. Thus, each human body is itself a Mercavah, a chariot of the Law. The four bodies of man are represented by the four heads of the living creature. The physical body is the earth or Taurus, which is seated in the heart. Therefore, the heart is the head of the bull in man. The next is the watery sign of Scorpio represented by the eagle which has its seat in the human spleen. The third is the fiery or emotional body of man, ruled by Leo, with its seat in the liver. The fourth head, that of the human being belongs to Aquarius, the principle of mind which has its seat in the brain. Each of these beasts goes a different way, that is, has its own surfaces and temperaments, yet together they form the chariot or Mercavah of the spirit.

In the Paracelsian theory, the earth is composed of four elements, earth, water, fire, and air. These, in turn, correspond with the four heads of the cherubim. They are, therefore, the elements or substances from which all bodies, that is chariots, are made. The hierarchies of the four corners or fixed signs, are called the builders, or the form builders, because they have control over the formative processes of nature. To them are given the streams of the elements which pouring through these hierarchies are distributed to form all corporeal natures. The cherubim are the four rivers that flow out of Eden making fertile the material universe. From their comixing are produced the vehicles for the manifestation of life. They are the four white horses that draw the chariot of Abraxas, the Gnostic Pantheos.

It is important to note that the four-headed creatures are represented in other religions with symbols of identical meaning. In India, the lord of the material universe, that is the world of the ancients personified, is Shiva, who is frequently represented with four heads. Brahma, manifested in the material universe through the Shivic principle, likewise, is depicted with four heads. He had a fifth head which was cut off during a battle in heaven. The story of the fifth head of Brahma is a delightful allegory concerning the fifth element, the azoth or quintessentia of alchemy—the universal mercury. In the Ezekiel account, the four creatures or elements carry in their midst the golden throne, the fifth element. Paracelsus says there is no greater mystery than the mystery of ether. Ether is truly the connective between the material and spiritual worlds, even as it is the connective by means of which every superphysical principle directs its material organisms.

The likeness of a man full of fire that rode upon the cherubim is, of course, spirit whether universal or individual which is supported and carried by the elements and their principles. The wheels full of eyes refer to the heavens, the planets, and constellations, particularly the great wheel of the zodiac which surrounds the earth and in which the cherubim turn. The universe itself is indeed the wheel within wheels. And in the midst of all the creatures sits the Ancient of Days, the Eternal One, the Axis of Law and Life, the Master of the Mysteries.

THE SUFFERINGS OF JOB

The book of Job may be called, without exaggeration, the finest and most significant book of the Bible. As literature it definitely excels any of the others. It is really a poem, although now presented in prose form in the King James version. There is a quality about the book of Job, a consistent excellence not to be found in any other of the Bible books. In theme, also, it transcends.

The book of Job is an initiation ritual, one of the finest expositions of the Mysteries to be found in the literature of the world. Unfortunately, its sublimity has been sensed by only a few of the most enlightened Bible students, and its inner meaning has been entirely ignored for centuries. All the average person knows about Job is that he had three perverse and worthless comforters who have become a byword for futile condolences.

The whole premise of the book of Job is exceedingly peculiar. Satan appearing before the footstool of God argues with the Creator concerning the piety of Job, a just, perfect, and upright man in whom there is no flaw. Satan insists that Job is pious only because of the plenty which he enjoys. The Lord then gives Satan the privilege of afflicting Job to prove that a good man in adversity still venerates his Lord. Whereupon, Satan, who has been walking up and down the earth, focuses his attention upon Job. Through the machinations of the evil one, Job is stripped of all his possessions, even his children being taken from him. But Job remains true, blessing the Lord that giveth and the Lord that taketh away. Another argument in heaven follows. Satan not discouraged, assures the Lord that if Job's flesh be corrupted, then surely the prophet will decry his maker. So, Job is visited with boils, corruptions of the flesh, and the three comforters.

The greater part of the book of Job is devoted to bits of advice given by the three comforters, and Job's reactions thereto. In his agony and torment, Job prays for death and release, but in his heart, he remains steadfast to his realization that the ways of God are mysterious, but that there is truth in all of them. At last, because Job preserved his faith throughout the sore afflictions that have been visited upon him, "the Lord blessed the latter end of Job more than his beginning." Wealth and honor were restored to him. "After this lived Job a hundred and forty years, and saw his sons, and his sons' sons, even four generations."

The roots of Goethe's Faust are laid in the story of Job. It is a story of struggle and achievement. It is exceedingly difficult for even an orthodox Christian to explain why God should pick out the most perfect of his prophets and turn him over to the tender mercies of Satan, to say nothing of Eliphaz the Temanite, Bildad the Shuhite, and Zophar the Naamathite. When understood as an esoteric fable setting forth acceptance into the Mysteries, the confusion is cleared away, Job is a neophyte, here depicted as a man of means and position. The Lord, in this case, is not God but the hierophant, the Master of the Secret House. Satan then assumes his correct position. He is the tester, the trier. In the ancient Mystery system, there was always a character who represented destruction, who sought to lure the neophyte away from the path of righteousness. He was frequently called the adversary.

Job, entering into the mysteries of initiation, must first renounce possessions. It is said of the Pythagorean community that "they possessed all in common and that no man had anything." Now a rich man being separated from his possessions usually suffers exceedingly. Furthermore, it was the duty of the Mystery School to discover that part of the neophyte's life which Was the weakest and assail him in that quarter. The student will remember how Socrates chastised Alcibiades for his love of wealth. And in India, even to this day, teachers force their disciples to perform those tasks most repugnant to them that they may overcome all likes and dislikes and achieve detachment. So, the initiator gave to Satan, the adversary, permission to strike Job in his weakest part, his wealth, to see whether the loss of things would destroy his vision or philosophy.

The seven sons and three daughters, like the seven thousand sheep and three thousand camels are entirely symbolical numbers. By the seven sons are signified his seven bodies or outward parts; and by the three daughters, his subjective or spiritual triad. But having been tested in his wealth, Job remained true. Thereupon, Satan is permitted to attack him in his honor, which is represented by the boils. Furthermore, he is tormented by three negative spirits who are sent to him in his hour of misery, even as in certain esoteric schools, the master is slain by three ruffians. The three are also the three degrees of the Mysteries which he must pass or rise above. By longing for death, Job infers that he repents of having attempted initiation at that time, but his spirit still survives and he continues on, passing through one infirmity after the other, until at last, he conquers himself and rises triumphantly from the ashes of his own sorrow.

He is rewarded by the return many times over of all he had lost. The Mysteries do not demand poverty, but they demand the right use of that which is possessed. Therefore, having become wise in all matters, Job received back his fortune, and with that his children, who, though dead, are conveniently born again of the same number and sex. Also, his cattle are multiplied. And he abodes in peace the rest of his days. The reader is not informed as to what occurred to either Satan or the three comforters who disappear when their work is completed.

This is by no means all of the story, but definitely is the key to it. The testing of Job is the testing of all men. Possibly the most difficult thing to explain is why a just man should be the one chosen for this misery. It should be remembered that the Mystery Schools accepted only the wisest and the most perfect, and then subjected them to ordeals of further testing before the secrets of the spiritual world should be revealed. If we look about us in life, we shall perceive as Job did, that the wicked seem to flourish and it is the just man who is stricken. This is part of the Divine Plan. The just man, having consecrated himself to the highest of his principles, is immediately confronted with karma and deluged with what seems to be adversity. In reality, this is not adversity, but the speeding up of evolution as the result of consecration to the spiritual life. More is expected of a man who is wise than of the man who is foolish. The older we grow, the more strength we have, and the more strength we have, the more sternly we are tested to prove that strength. But no man is tested beyond his capacity. Therefore, the Lord says to Satan that he may afflict Job, but that he may not take his life.

Satan is not a spirit of destruction. There is no essential evil in the universe. Our present form of the devil is merely derived from the Greek nature god Pan. As Goethe says, Mephistopheles, or Satan, "is part of the power that still works for good while ever scheming ill." Satan is really karma, but he is more than that. He is that temptation from which arises strength. When the Mysteries were celebrated in ancient Egypt, there was an evil spirit called Typhon or Set who brought about the death of the good Osiris. It is the red Set that has given us our concept of the devil, but Set was nothing but the material world, the ground of man's temptation, and also the environment in which he gains immortality through self-discipline. Therefore, Set or Satan, is the divine opportunity; the world into which we come in ignorance but from which we depart in wisdom. It is the obstacle that is ever building strength, it is that whole field of difficulty which, overcome, makes us master of our own life.

MELCHIZEDEK

The 18th verse of the 14th chapter of Genesis reads: "And Melchizedek king of Salem brought forth bread and wine: and he was the priest of the most high God." The meeting of Abraham and Melchizedek seems to be the first statement of the Eucharist. The word Melchizedek, is believed to mean king of righteousness, but this translation is entirely exoteric. In the old Chaldean Hebrew, Melchizedek, means the authority of Sedek, or Sedek is king. Therefore, Sedek is king of Salem which can mean either peace or a heaped-up place. The city of Jerusalem is built upon a number of hills. The word Sedek comes from the Egyptian. The god Sedek was the father of the artificer-gods of Egypt. Faber in his great work on the Noahic cycle, the Cabiri, says that in the Phoenician and Samothracian rites, the seven Cabiri, that is the seven planetary gods that turn or move about the sun, are the children of Sedek. So Melchizedek is father Sedek, the father of the planets and the Cabirian artificers. Thus, Sedek it the sun. We have the same symbolism as with Moses, the letters of whose name, if rearranged, form the name of the sun, Samach. Moses, the red-haired man and Melchizedek the king, the first priest, are both sun-men.

Now we understand why Melchizedek was his own father and mother and why he is the founder of the eternal priesthood. We also understand why Christ is likened unto Melchizedek and why he is called a priest after the order of Melchizedek. The sun gives light to all the world, Christ lighteth every man that cometh into the world. Therefore, Christ is a light symbol, and all light is derived from the great light, the sun whose temple is eternal in the heavens. The sons of the sun are the light-bringers, the prophets and teachers, for as the sun dispels the darkness of night, so the prophets dispel the darkness of ignorance and assume their legitimate place as servants of light.

Yours sincerely,

Manly P. Hall

LETTER NO. 7

Dear Friend,

THE SECRET DOCTRINE IN THE BIBLE
THE NEW TESTAMENT

With this letter we begin the study of the New Testament. The twenty-seven books of the New Testament are concerned principally with the life and teachings of Christ and the ministry of his apostles. The exception to this is the book of Revelation which derives its inspiration from the metaphysics of the Egyptians.

The Old Testament was written in Hebrew and belongs particularly to the tradition of the Jewish people. The New Testament was written originally in Greek, although no manuscripts of the first or second centuries A. D. are known to exist. There was a wholesale destruction of these early manuscripts during and after the Council of Nicea A.D. 325.

The gravest doubts exist as to the authorship of the gospels of the New Testament. The encyclopedia Britannica acknowledges not only these doubts, but admits that there is no proof of any kind that the Gospels were written by the men whose names have been affixed to them in more recent time.

The oldest existing codices of the New Testament reveal considerable change and amendment. The King James version omits a number of passages of a controversial nature, particularly such as would cause doubt to arise concerning the uniqueness or the infallibility of the Christian faith. The King James Bible was published first in 1611 under the patronage of James 1 of England. The actual translations were made by a number of scholars from leading universities. They were elderly men many of whom died before the book of Psalms was reached. The work was undertaken during the most corrupt period of English education. The principal university records of the time consist of the amount of beer drunk by the student body. There is a story, possibly apocryphal but with a ring of truth about it, that King James' final instructions to the translators were in substance as follows: Where the new Translations agree with accepted tradition, use them; where they do not, conform to the popular tradition.

When the manuscript was completed, it was given into the hands of Lord Bacon who is responsible for its present literary excellence. He achieved the impressiveness now evident in the book largely by taking liberties with the text. As a result, the Bible student is not justified in accepting the King James version as an infallible production, or in believing that the divine dictates were revealed originally in the King's English.

In addition to the accepted books of the New Testament, there are a number of apocryphal writings and associated works which have been excluded from the Bible for a number of reasons. In some cases, these books are highly imaginative flights, and in others they are far too pointed for distribution among the laity. Several important variants of the Gospels and Epistles still exist in European libraries, but there seems to be no great haste to translate or edit these codices for general circulation. The most perplexing and comparatively unsolvable mystery with which the Christian theologian is faced is the almost complete lack of historical evidence concerning the life of Christ. If we except a few palpable forgeries, our knowledge of the life of Christ is based principally upon the accounts given in the Gospels. It is safe to say that thousands of books dealing with the life of Christ have been published since the invention of printing, but only on rare occasions do the authors attempt a critical scholarship.

The Bible itself contains a number of discrepancies on the subject, some of which we shall point out as we proceed. It is not our intention to state that Jesus Christ never lived, but we are forced in the cause of honesty to affirm that there is no adequate contemporaneous evidence to support the Gospel stones. We feel, therefore, that the true significance of the Gospels lies, not in their historical parts, but, in their mystical parts. The Jesus of Galilee may or may not have lived, but we agree entirely with St. Paul that this is not of first importance, rather it is the "Christ in you" that is the hope of glory.

THE BIRTH AND CHILDHOOD OF JESUS

The life of Jesus as given in the Gospels is so familiar to every class of reader that it seems unnecessary to summarize this account. We shall devote our space entirely to a consideration of problem and interpretation.

There is great controversy concerning the actual date of the birth of Jesus. Herod, Tetrarch of Galilee, died B.C. 4. This is embarrassing because it is quite evident that he could not have ordered the "slaughter of the innocents." The account of Joseph and Mary going up to Bethlehem to be registered according to the laws of Rome also is unfortunate. Rome only exercised the law of registry on one occasion, and that was during the reign of Quirinus, (Gr. Cyrenus) about ten years after the death of Herod. Thus, we have an interval of ten years of uncertainty which every educated theologian knows but seldom discusses.

The reader should remember that the Fathers of the early Church were themselves in considerable discord over the time of the birth of Jesus. Various years were suggested in an attempt to reconcile theology and history. This finally was given up as hopeless and the debate narrowed itself to the consideration of the winter solstice and the vernal equinox as possible birth dates. The Church fought for five hundred years to decide which date was right. The decision was handed down in the end by a process of balloting. It is evident that the problem was astronomical. Was the sun born at the winter solstice or the vernal equinox? These were the most sacred dates of the pagan world.

There is an early Christian system of reckoning by means of the lunar cycle of nineteen years. This is called the epact. Its calculations are based upon the birth time of Jesus. Tracing back through the epact, it would appear that Jesus was born at the conjunction of the sun and moon on the 24th of March at 1:30 in the morning, at the meridian of Jerusalem.

Necessity entered into the problem of commemorating holy days. Meetings of the Christians were forbidden in the city of Rome. One of the principal feasts of the Romans fell near the winter solstice. The Christians met at this time because the vigilance of the Romans was relaxed during the celebration of their feast. This seems to be the origin of the observance of Christmas on the 25th of December. Problems of this would confound any system of theology. In simple fact and substance, no one knows either the day, month, or year of the Nativity.

Searching in this maze of theological oratory and historical discrepan-

THE BIRTH AND CHILDHOOD OF JESUS   91

cies, we arrive at the probable date of the historical Jesus. In the Talmud of the Jews, we learn that Jehoshua Ben Panthira was born about the year B.C. 120 in the reign of the Jewish King Alexander Jannes. This man lived, was a rabbin of considerable influence, a reactionist, and was finally stoned to death for heresy. He was a disciple of the great Jehoshua Ben Prachia, a member of the Jewish Sanhedrin, a man who had arisen from the state of a rabbin to a place of high honor among the orthodox Jews.

About the year B.C. 100, Jehoshua Ben Panthira, then about twenty years of age, accompanied his master Ben Prachia to Egypt to escape King Alexander's persecution of the rabbins. The statement that Jesus studied with the Egyptian priests is to be found not only in the Talmudic writings, but in certain early manuscripts of the Christian Gospels. The Talmud states that this Jesus, or Jehoshua, travelled to Egypt with Ben Prachia to study sorcery, so that he became a miracle worker, gained the power of healing the sick, and practiced illusions. There is an old manuscript which dates from the revision during the Byzantine Period, centuries before the King James version, which was for time in the possession of the secret order of the Knights Templars of Jerusalem. The sixth chapter, 42nd verse, of St. John intimates the journey of Jesus into Egypt. In the King James version Verse 42 reads: "And they said, is not this Jesus, the son of Joseph, whose father and mother we know? how is it then he sayeth, I come down from heaven?" The manuscript reads: "And they said, is not this Jesus, the son of Joseph, whose father and mother we know? how is it then that he sayeth, I came down from heaven? Is it because he has dwelt among the Greeks that he comes thus to speak with us? What is there in common between what he has learned from the Egyptians and what our fathers have taught us?"

By leaving out the last part of this verse, the life of Jesus between his thirteenth and his thirtieth years had been left empty and mysterious. Also, his connection with the great pagan systems of learning has been withheld from his followers by an unworthy stratagem.

In the Talmud, in the Hebrew gloss upon Ecclesiastes, (Midras koheleth) there is another mention of Jehoshua or Jesus as follows: "It happened that a serpent bit R. Eleasar Ben Damah, and James, a man of the village Secania, came to heal him in the name of Jehoshua Ben Panthira." The Talmud adds further: "Jehoshua was bewitched, raised up, and turned Israel away from her fathers." After their return from Egypt, it appears that Jehoshua and his master Ben Prachia quarreled, parted, and never met again.

In the Talmud, Jesus is called also Hammassiah as a prefix or forename.

It is derived by combining the Egyptian word Ammon and Messiah. It also is said that Jehoshua, the son of Panthira and Stada was stoned to death as a wizard in the city of Lydda, and afterwards his body was hung on a tree. His death occurred about B.C. 70.

The attitudes of the early Church, Fathers may be summarized in the words of two of the proudest pillars of the faith, Tertullian and St. Augustine. Tertullian was one of the three great North African bishops. He is the great authority of the Church, unquestioned upon any ground whatever. He is the very stuff from which orthodoxy is made. To quote him: "I maintain that the son of God died; well, that is wholly credible, because it is monstrously absurd—I maintain that having been buried, he rose again; and that I take to be absolutely true, because it is manifestly impossible." From this fine example of Tertullian logic, we pass to St. Augustine who says: "I would never have believed the Gospels unless the authority of the Church had induced me to do it." In the presence of such illustrious company, we feel that our doubts on certain matters are no less reasonable than theirs. From extensive research I am convinced that regardless of the historical controversy, our true Christian mysticism lies not in the acceptance of historical facts, but in the inward spiritual perception of certain divine truths.

THE MYSTICAL CHRIST

In the first chapter of the Gospel according to St. John it is written: "In the beginning was the Word, and the Word was with God, and the Word was God." It is further written: "And the Word was made flesh, and dwelt among us." It is universally acknowledged that the Gospel attributed to John is the most mystical of the four. It omits the genealogies and the account of the Nativity, and assumes that Jesus Christ was the Son of God, the incarnation of the divine fiat. From the first chapter of John, we gain a profound knowledge of the metaphysical elements in the Christian Mysteries. It is almost certain that this work was influenced by the Gnostic tradition which flourished in both Syria and Egypt during the first century A.D. Gnosticism derived its authority directly from the Gospels and the apostles, and maintained that it possessed the secret key of esoteric Christianity. Several mystical groups flourished in Syria at the same time. The Cabalistic Sect was arising among the Jews, the Nazarenes arid the Therapeutae were represented by itinerant teachers who wandered up and down the countryside. The Essenes had monasteries along the shores of the Dead Sea and by the lakes of Upper Egypt. Each of these schools had its prophet, its dogma, and its arcana. The Syrian orders were mostly Messianic. They were waiting, one and all, for a king to be born in Israel according to the prophecies and the Scriptures. He should be born of the house of David, and should rescue Israel from bondage to Rome.

The Roman governors of Syria considered their appointments to this barren country little better than political exile. There were constant uprisings, rebellions, and intrigues. Rome held on to Syria principally from motives of pride. Rome never relinquished anything. Financially, their military occupation was a wasteful expense bringing no return. The local Jewish princes toadied to both Israel and Rome, attempting to maintain their own positions at all costs. Rome never was able to subdue their Jewish colonials and left most of the administration of local affairs in the hands of Jewish tetrarchs.

It was in the midst of this general disorder and dissatisfaction that the Christian ministry was announced, or at least, such is the modern story. There is much mystery concerning the origin of Christianity. The Fathers of the Church of the second century seemed to be no better informed on the matter than those of the twentieth century, the general consensus of opinion being that the "King of Kings" was born to the Jews, preached along the sea of Galilee, died on Calvary, and in the person of his apostles and followers, later overthrew the Roman Empire.

It is my belief that the present Christian faith is built upon the teachings of certain Syrian sects, particularly the Essene and the Nazarene. These sects were distinguished for their virtue and propriety, and of all the Jewish communities, they alone made claim to extensive scholarship. Roman governors and officers stationed among the Jews engaged Essenes as tutors for their children. This order claimed descent from the Greek master Pythagoras who had visited Mt. Lebanon and founded a cult there in the fifth century B.C. The Nazirs also occupied a prominent position. They were bound together by vows and certain rituals. They had an oath that they would cut neither hair nor beard until the coming of the Messiah. It should be remembered also that the Jewish mysticism of that time had been considerably influenced by the captivities in Egypt and Babylon.

Somewhere among these sects appeared the doctrine of the "Word made flesh." There can be no question but that the Egyptian god Horus the younger was the pattern used in creating the Messianic character. It is entirely possible that our story of the life of Christ is the account of a neophyte passing through the degrees of a secret order. We know that such initiation rituals have given us our mythologies of Greece, Rome, Egypt, India, and China. The Grecian gods and Roman heroes were personages of an ancient religious ceremonial. A copy of the book of the dead was found recently in which this presumed account of the soul's wandering in Amenti was marginally decorated with prompter's notes, proving beyond question that it was a drama actually portrayed by living people. If the death and resurrection of Osiris was a play performed on rare occasions with profound solemnity, why may not the Christian drama be of like nature?

The medieval Church perpetuated the ritualistic aspects of Christian mysticism in their mystery plays. These dramas were presented on certain feast days on the wide porches of the cathedrals. The plays usually depicted incidents in the life of Christ, the life of the Virgin, or the trials of the apostles. Sometimes the plays were interpreted by readers who stood in the high stone pulpits near the church door. Some of the plays took the form of processionals, but usually they were episodical.

The explanation now given for these plays is that the illiteracy of the people and the numerous dialectical difficulties in language made preaching and teaching difficult, whereas the visual enactment was understandable to all. Nevertheless, their close similarity to the ancient mystery plays is a strong point in favor of their direct descent from the pagan initiation dramas.

If this be the case, and certainly such an interpretation is the most meaningful that can be given to the story, we readily understand why historicity is wanting. It would be impossible to give the birth date of Dionysius, Apollo, Odin, Vishnu, or these other "divine beings" inasmuch as they were personifications of universal forces contrived as a means of revealing them through legend and fable.

It is very possible that the early Church Fathers, seeding desperately for a concrete human being on which to hang the fabric of their faith, picked Jehoshua Ben Panthira as the nearest parallel to be found among the Jewish rabbins. Armed with, this small fragment of history, they proceeded to correlate the two, building in a little here, and removing some contradictory fragment there, until, lo, and behold! the "King of Kings" is a Nazarene, in spite of the popular opinion that nothing good could come out of Nazareth.

This further explains why Helena, the mother of Constantine, within three hundred years after the death of Jesus was unable to find in all of Jewry any man who had even heard of him. According to the story, she finally came upon one aged man who claimed to have heard that Jesus had lived.

He took her to an old Roman execution field where excavations revealed a number of crosses. When the whole matter had been settled to everyone's satisfaction, Constantine, to show his extreme veneration, had one of the passion nails pounded into a bit for his horse. This, in the presence of the fact that nails had not been invented at that time, shows us just about where we stand. We might add that another one of the nails was melted into the iron crown of Hungary.

We conclude that the Christ of the Gospels was a symbolical personage, created in the adytum of some ancient temple to personify man's whole search for truth, and that Truth itself, for the following reasons:

1. There is no satisfactory proof of the physical existence of Christ.

2. Christ is associated definitely with the solar myth.

3. The miracles of Jesus could not have taken place without historical recognition.

4. Heretics were not crucified under the Roman law, this penalty being reserved for murderers, robbers, and highwaymen.

5. Herod, Tetrarch of Galilee, died 4 B.C.

6. The only Roman registration of the Jews was under Quirinus, A.D. 6.

7. The slaughter of the innocents did not take place.

8. There is no proof that the Gospels were written by the men whose names they bear.

9. The early Roman Church was in no agreement as to the life of Christ, Irenaeus claiming that he lived to old age.

10. It is exceedingly doubtful if St. Peter was ever in Rome.

11. The golden legend by Voragine is filled with impossible and absurd legends, most of which have been believed as literal truths for centuries.

All of which indicates the quality of criticism with which these religious subjects have been considered. From these, and a mass of other material contradictory and controversial, we are inclined to question the literal Christ as an instrument of spiritual power, and to see in the story a mystical exposition of divine spiritual truths.

INTERPRETATION

If we consider the Gospel account in the light of comparative religion, we shall find that there is very little contained therein not to be found in the great religious systems of the pagan world. It is written in the Bible that Mary the wife of Joseph received a vision in which it was foretold that a son should be born to her, she should call him Jesus, and he would deliver Israel from sin. It is most significant that the name of the Virgin should be Mary. There are important phonetic associations. The Latin word mare means the sea. Of course, the word virgin also means pure—and virgin mare means pure sea. In pagan symbolism the sea is the natural symbol of illusion because of the reflecting quality of water. Mary is Isis, the Egyptian goddess of the Mysteries whose veil no man might lift. She is the virgin Sophia, the Mother of Adepts; she is Diana of the Ephesians, the mater deorum of the Romans; she is Istar, Astarte, Mylitta.

The Annunciation has its parallel in the legends of the Aztec Indians. Quetzalcoatl, god of the winds and of the sky, whose symbol was the cross and who shed his blood for the sins of his people, was born of Sochiquetzal in the land of the seven colors. An angelic spirit descended from the constellation of Orion and told his mother that she should bear a son who should save his people.

Mary the mother of Jesus, Maya the mother of Buddha, have an identical significance. They are the womb of the Mysteries from whom are born the sons of light, the redeemers, the saviors of men. He who enters the temple and having perfected himself in the sacred wisdom emerges therefrom between the pillars of the porch, is indeed born again out of the Great Mother, Wisdom. Therefore, he is a son of Wisdom, in Egypt, the son of the hawk and the son of the widow—Isis mourning for Osiris.

In ancient time, the coming of a new adept was announced from the portico of the temple. The god-men, the twice-born ones, were no longer as ordinary mortals, they were the objects of a universal veneration, the most honored of mortals because they were the closest to Truth. These adepts are called "sons of the silent mother" in some of the ancient writings. They bore witness before men of the light. They were frequently referred to as the "sons of God."

Our word college comes from the ancient collegium which was a society of artisans bound together by vows. Our word gymnasium is derived from one of the names for the temple of wisdom. The institution is the mother of its graduates. The same thought survives to this day in our exoteric system of education. In the term alma mater, the university is acknowledged as the mother of its graduates. The Annunciation, therefore, announces the coming of an initiate. His star has been seen. He has come forth from the portals of the House of Wisdom, the virgin mother of the wise. She is the one who, though her sons be many, is still a virgin.

Joseph took his wife Mary down to Bethlehem to be registered. There was no room in the inn and the travelers were lodged in the stable or grotto. It appears from the account that the stable was partly a natural cave. The present grotto of the Nativity shown to visitors at Bethlehem is definitely a cavern in natural rock. This is the most important part of the symbolism. Eaber in his Cabiri has reproduced a picture of a cave of the Mysteries as a frontispiece.

Mithras, the Persian Christ, was born in a cavern. Caves are symbols of both the womb and the tomb, or birth and death. Primitive peoples believed that their ancestors lived under the earth in caverns where they celebrated and feasted. Mounds were the domes of the palaces of the dead. A pyramid is a highly perfected mound, containing rooms for either burial or initiation, or both. The Southwestern Indians of America still believe that the gods dwell under the earth, that they themselves came out of the earth in the beginning, and also, that the souls of the dead return again to the underworld. Among the Indians in the vicinity of the Grand Canyon, there are legends to the effect that this great natural abyss led downward into the world of the spirits. Volcanoes were similarly honored and for the same reason. In their kivas or houses of initiation, the Hopis dig a small chimney-like hole down into the earth believing that through this opening the gods can hear their deliberations. The belief that the dead live under the earth and that an initiation into the mysteries is a symbolic death, caused the rites of the pagan mysteries to be given nocturnally and in weird, subterranean places, frequently crypts.

The infant Jesus was born in a manger surrounded by animals. These animals merely represent the animal world, or the material universe, wherein most mortals dwell in the state of dumb, driven cattle. There may be another link in this part of the story. In the Egyptian Mysteries, candidates were surrounded by masked priests who bore over their faces the masks of various animals. One of the most frequently used was that of the bull or ox. These masked priests represented the temptations of the animal world with which the neophyte is repeatedly tested.

Jesus was born in a manger. The manger is the feeding trough from which the animal nature eats of the grain and seed, particularly the seed of wheat, the life-bestower, which has long been the symbol of the savior god. This is a survival of the agricultural cult of very primitive time. The death and resurrection story belong to the agrarian period of early humanity. After thousands of years, the cult of the wheat seed descended even to St. Paul who likening the seed to Christ says: "That which thou sowest is not quickened, except it die." (1 Cor. 15:36. Read the entire chapter for further examples of the seed symbolism.) Tithing survives from the same period. Some prophets of ancient days realizing the wastefulness of man decreed that ten percent of the seed should be dedicated to the god of increase and should be put away for the next sowing, for if ten percent of the seed were not returned to the earth, there would be famine and sorrow in the land.

The Star of Bethlehem is susceptible of numerous interpretations. Several writers have attempted to prove that a conjunction of Jupiter and Saturn heralded the Nativity. The Gnostic interpretation is probably the nearest to the truth. They taught that the star was not seen by ordinary mortals, but only by such as possessed inward vision. The star was the soul of the adept descending from the spheres of light, the higher eons. At initiation, the higher self is united with the mortal nature. This luminous over-soul, the Anthropos, full of light and shining unto the ends of creation, descended through the substances of the invisible planes and came to rest finally in the body of the new adept. This concept is distinctly pagan. After the death of Julius Caesar, a comet was seen. The Romans regarded this comet as the soul of Caesar ascending to the abode of the blessed. This interpretation is more or less inferred by the Gospel account. Only three wise men came to worship at the manger of the babe, and these came because they had seen his star. The Gnostics taught that the soter, or Savior, descended through an infinity of eons, lighting each one, falling like a flame from the sky. In modern esoteric systems, the aura or subtle body plays the part of the star. From this aura it is possible to tell the spiritual estate of man.

Three wise men, kings of Eastern lands, came to Bethlehem, following the star. They brought gold, frankincense and myrrh as offerings to the newborn babe. Gold is the symbol of mind and of power. Frankincense is the symbol of emotion and beauty. And myrrh is the symbol of the body because it was used in the embalming of the dead. The wise men belonged to the three races to signify that all living things adore the ever-living Truth. The wise kings are the three lower eons of the Gnostics, the symbols of the inferior parts of man's own nature. Together they make up the personality composed of thought, emotion, and matter. This lower man humbles itself before the incarnate Word and gives allegiance and recognition to the spiritual self.

The Immaculate Conception constitutes one of the principal problems of the Church. The acceptance of the Virgin Birth of Christ is advanced usually as an absolute prerequisite to salvation. There are several possible interpretations. Buddha was born through the right side of his mother which might signify a Caesarian birth, a term based upon the fact that Julius Caesar was so born. At the time of Caesar this was recognized already as a symbol of extraordinary excellence, an omen of greatness. Most of the savior gods are born of an immaculate conception, through which circumstance they gain an especial esteem. Of course, in the dictionary the word immaculate means clean or without blemish, and in itself infers no miraculous or metaphysical circumstance. The word assumes a supernatural significance only in the terminology of the Church.

Ancient peoples desiring to honor their prophets and teachers frequently ascribed to them some supernatural origin. Even Mohammed's birth was accompanied by wonders. But these wonders belong entirely to the imagination of the pious.

It is intimated that the mother of Jesus had other sons and daughters to whom no supernatural qualities are attributed. There is no factual foundation for a belief that Jesus was conceived in any other than a normal manner. A parallel for this is found in the birth of Pythagoras. Although his father and mother are clearly mentioned, it is stated by his most enthusiastic admirers that he was conceived by the specter of the god Apollo which they themselves called a "holy ghost." This was not intended literally, but rather astrologically, as he was born under the sign Leo which was ruled by the sun god Apollo.

In the Gospel story, Herod is made out as a man of despicable villainy. In truth, he was a mild, kindly person, very solicitous of the welfare of his people, and more or less a nonentity occupying a wellnigh hopeless position. He appears no better and no worse than the average prince of his time. He was beset constantly with uprisings and turmoil directed not against Rome but against himself. It is this man who has been immortalized as the personification of all corruption.

The Jewish hatred for everything Roman may have inspired a general dislike for Herod, but it is probable that he was simply chosen in the Christian drama to play the part of evil because he fitted approximately into the desired plan. The origin of Herod's massacre of the innocents is twofold. First, in India where Krishna is smuggled away as an infant when the evil king causes the murder of the firstborn. And second, in the story of Ben Panthira being forced to flee into Egypt to escape the Jewish persecution of the rabbins. The Krishna story in India is centuries older than the Christian account, but it is practically identical with it. The slaughter of the innocents belongs definitely in the class of apocrypha. (See Mathew 2:16 for the account.)

The Romans were good historians, and so was Josephus. The slaughter of the firstborn of a whole province never could have escaped history. Early Christian theologians have declared that the innocents slaughtered by Herod represented the saints martyred for Christ. But even this fails to solve the mystery.

Let us think then in the terms of the Mystery ritual. Christ represents truth and wisdom. Herod is cast in the role of ignorance and evil. Ignorance and perversion realize that in the presence of truth they must fail. Therefore, they set about to discover and destroy truth. But what is truth? and where is it to be found? The institute of Pythagoras at Crotona was burned by a disgruntled and rejected candidate. The master escaped but died soon after, probably crucified by his enemies. Under the guidance of Rome, the religious and political sects of Syria were as far as possible broken up, their members killed or sent into exile. Take for example the case of Simeon ben Jachoia who was forced to hide in a cave for years. The breaking up and destruction of the old Mystery Schools and the persecution and martyrdom of their disciples is one of the key interpretations of this fable. In Revelation the woman, the Mysteries, is sent out into the desert which describes the scattering of the initiates into the Arabian desert. By analogy, this also represents the efforts to destroy truth in society and in man by the cunning contrivances of ignorance and perversion.

Yours sincerely,

Manly P. Hall

LETTER NO. 8

Dear Friend,

THE SECRET DOCTRINE IN THE BIBLE - THE FLIGHT INTO EGYPT

The flight of the Holy Family into Egypt to escape the persecutions of Herod is described in Matt. 2:13-14. This incident appears to be derived in part from the journey of Jehoshua Ben Panthira as given in the Talmud. In the Gospel account, the flight into Egypt is inserted during the infancy of Jesus to prevent the pious reader from inferring that Jesus was a student of Egyptian philosophy. The date of the return of Jesus from Egypt is not given, and this has led uninitiated readers, to the conclusion that he returned while still a child. Such a conclusion is not necessarily true.

The New Testament writers and editors in their efforts to establish the divinity of Jesus, have advanced him as the Messiah promised in the writings of the Jewish prophets. We are assured that Matt. 2:15 is the literal fulfillment of Hosea 11:1; "When Israel was a child, then I loved him, and called my son out of Egypt." The context of Hosea hardly justifies any analogy to the New Testament account. There can be no doubt, however, that the compilers of the New Testament had the older documents in mind and, wherever possible, perpetrated many pious frauds to force the New Testament into a fulfillment of the Old.

The true origin of the Messianic mystery is to be found in the secret doctrines of the Egyptians. Isis conceived of the Holy Ghost a son, Horus the younger. Typhon, the principle of evil, sought to destroy the child, so Isis bore him away and hid him among the reeds in the swamps by the edge of the Nile. It was this same son Horus who, growing to manhood, led the army of the enlightened in a great war against Typhon, destroying him utterly. This war is the Armageddon of the Scriptures. The Egyptian allegory means that Horus (wisdom) is concealed by Isis (the initiated priesthood) from Typhon (the profane and corrupt) so that only those who have been accepted into the Mysteries can discover the arcana. Horus leads the initiates in the great war against evil. Thus, wisdom overcomes ignorance, and the earth ultimately comes to a state of peace and happiness.

It is evident that Horus was a prototype of Christ. The infant Horus, in the form of Harpocrates, is depicted with one lock of hair falling over his left shoulder, his finger to his lips, and crippled in his lower parts. Images of him were placed at the entrances to the Egyptian temples. He occasionally was called the god of silence. Like other Messianic gods, Horus was born under the sign of Capricorn, the home of the ancient one, called in Egypt the constellation of the stable. Among the names bestowed upon Horus-Harpocrates were: "the Prince of Peace," "the Ever-coming One," "the Merciful," "the Immortal" "the Hostage of those who have sinned" and "the Resurrected One."

Horus was not only the son of Osiris, but actually the embodiment of his father, posthumously conceived. Osiris, the father-god, lived again in his own son and was truly one with him. From this we learn that Truth (Osiris the elder) is one with the Secret Doctrine or Wisdom (Horus the younger). Truth abides in Wisdom and Wisdom is a manifestation of Truth. The early Christian Church, through the process of councils and synods, determined that there was no difference between the proper person of God and the proper person of Christ—they later added the Holy Ghost. This agrees entirely with the statement of Egyptian mythology that Osiris was his own father and his own son. Osiris was born in Horus that he might be his own avenger. As lord of Amentet, Osiris was also the Holy Spirit, the judge of the quicks and the dead.

Osiris-Horus attacks Typhon, the Adversary. Typhon is the "red ass" depicted in Egyptian art either as an ass or as a composita made up of the body of a hippopotamus and the head of a crocodile. After conquering Typhon, Horus binds the spirit of evil to his chariot and rides upon the body of the creature. This symbolism is preserved in the New Testament in the story of Jesus riding into Jerusalem on the ass's colt.

THE CHILDHOOD OF JESUS

In Egypt the life of the individual was divided into three important parts—infancy, adolescence, and maturity. Adolescence began at the twelfth year when the child-lock of hair was cut off. Maturity was achieved at thirty. It is significant that the New Testament contains no mention of the life of Jesus between his infancy and his twelfth year, nor after that until his thirtieth year. By analogy, then, Jesus represents the normal human being fulfilling all the parts of the life of a man, for even among the Jews, a rabbin could not teach until he was thirty.

The life of Jesus between his infancy and his thirtieth year undoubtedly was devoted to travel and study. It is a fallacy to believe that the teachings attributed to Jesus are a direct and unique revelation. All of his teachings can be traced to older religions and the faiths of other peoples. Prominent among the sources of Christian doctrines are the religions of India, Egypt, Greece, Persia, and the earlier Jews. A record recently has been found that indicates a visit to Tibet. Also, there are legends about him in India. His journeys among the Greeks are rather well established. There is no proof whatsoever that Jesus did not receive religious training, not only in distant lands, but among his own people. There were several sects among the Jews, any one of which could have been his mentor. Even in the New Testament his learning in the doctrines of the Jews is acknowledged.

JESUS BAPTIZED BY JOHN

In Matt. 3 is related the preachings of John the Baptizer. Many were baptized by John throughout all of Judea and the regions about the Jordan. The compilers of the Gospels make him cry out to the peoples, "Repent ye: for the kingdom of heaven is at hand." In Matt. 3:4 there is a description of John: "And the same John had his raiment of camel's hair, and a leathern girdle about his loins; and his meat was locusts and wild honey."

John the Baptist dies a victim to the hate of Herodias. He is decapitated and his head brought to the daughter of Herodias on a charger. Incidentally, Salome was the favorite of Herod and begged this favor from him more than thirty years after he was dead. Therefore, we may suspect that the account is allegorical and should not be taken as historically significant.

The death of John has several interpretations. It can mean the breaking up and scattering of a religious sect by the execution of its "heads" or leaders. It can mean also the passing of an old religious system, in substance, the pagan world. John is the link between the Old and the New Testaments, the old and the new dispensations. The death of John coincident with the ministry of Christ is a cunningly conceived artifice to advance the cause of early Christianity. Also, John represents the animal man who must give way to the divine man. He represents the purification that must precede illumination. He is the human soul itself crying in the wilderness.

The crest of the Roman Popes includes two crossed keys, one of silver and the other of gold. The silver key is said to unlock the mysteries of Israel, the Cabala of the Old Testament; and the golden key is said to unlock the mysteries of the New Testament, the Cabala of the Messianic dispensation. Thus, even the Roman Church acknowledges that a key is symbolically necessary and that certain mysteries are hidden from the profane to be unlocked only by the two-faced Janus, keeper of the keys.

According to the old tradition, the Secret Doctrine of the pagan world, the exoteric religion was called the body of the faith, and the esoteric or concealed parts were called the head. Therefore, the loss of the secret tradition of the ancient world is represented by the decapitation of John. In the Greek Mysteries it is Orpheus whose body is torn to pieces by the frenzy of the Ciconian women, but whose head continues to give oracles. In Matt. 3:11 John is caused to say: "I indeed baptize you with water unto repentance: but he that cometh after me is mightier than I, whose shoes I am not worthy to bear: he shall baptize you with the Holy Ghost, and with fire." It is unlikely that the Nazarene John ever said any such words, but it is necessary to the Messianic story that he should acknowledge the sovereignty of the Messiah. Another example of a similar legend was the quaint belief of the early Church fathers that on the day of nativity all the oracles of the pagan world ceased and a voice cried out from the depths: "Great Pan is dead."

Pan was a sylvan god. He lived among the reeds by the rivers, and played upon his pipes. He was a wild forest spirit, Jupiter in the form of nature. Pan very closely parallels John the Baptizer who also dwelt in the wilderness and was dressed in the skins of beasts. As Pan represented nature and nature's law, likewise John represented the material sphere, nature in its quest for Truth. Both Pan and John died, so the legends say, because nature gives way to law, and law gives way to Truth. It is a true spiritual mystery that the lower world dies in that man who has been lifted up into communion with the real.

When Jesus insists that he be baptized by John, the inner meaning is that Jesus insists upon being accepted into the old dispensation. He brought not a new law, but a fulfillment of the law. By accepting baptism, he fulfilled the law and the prophets. In this sense, John the Baptist is Israel that had wandered long in the wilderness; and words are put into his mouth by the early Gospel writers for their own ends. He is made to acknowledge the new dispensation which in true character he never would have done had he been a Syrian hermit. By John baptizing with water, Israel is represented as possessing the Lesser Mysteries; and Christ by baptizing with fire is made to represent the Greater Mysteries. The whole account is almost certainly apocryphal, but it is necessary to the general development of the story and establishment of the Christian position in this drama of the ages.

THE MARRIAGE FEAST AT CANA

The Gospel according to St. John 2:1-11 describes the first miracle that was wrought by Jesus, the changing of water into wine. By this miracle Jesus is associated with Bacchus or Dionysius, the vine god. Exoterically, Bacchus was a symbol of the grape, esoterically, of the sun and the divine soul. Bacchus drives a chariot drawn by panthers. We should not forget that Jehoshua Ben Panthira means Jehoshua, son of the panther. The first miracle-related of Bacchus is that he changed water into wine at a wedding feast. This miracle was performed more than a thousand years before the birth of Jesus. The Christian communion cup is nothing but the chalice of Bacchus whose blood was symbolized by the juice of the vine. The I H S embroidered on the Christian altar cloths is the monogram of Bacchus. Incidentally, Bacchus was canonized in both his forms as St. Bacchus and St. Dionysius.

Even Eusebius, the great liar of Christendom, acknowledged that the miracles associated with Christ and his apostles were derived from the attributes of pagan gods, a dangerous and seldom studied admission. In the old frescoes and mosaics, the god Bacchus is usually depicted riding on a donkey. He is surrounded by the bacchantes carrying flowers and fruits, with grape leaves twisted in their hair. The Greek form of Bacchus was a young and beautifully proportioned man with long curling hair hanging on his shoulders. He carried the thyrsus and should never be confused with the Roman form of the god, the rotund and tipsy Silenus. The real Bacchus was a god of the Mysteries and not a wine-bibber.

It is interesting to consider the amount of wine that is supposed to have been produced by the miracle at Cana. According to the best data available, this would have been approximately 19 gallons.

In the Greek rituals of Bacchus, great urns of water were carried into the temple and placed before the altar of the god. The doors of the temple then were carefully locked and sealed, and guarded against deceit. The next morning when the seals upon the doors had been broken and the priests had admitted the multitude to the temple, the water had been changed to wine. This wine was then distributed to the people in a sacred ceremony in which it was taught that those who partook of this wine drank the blood of the god.

A wedding feast frequently symbolizes the gathering of the initiates of an order, the wedding garments being the robes of the initiates. The key to this whole miracle at Cana can be traced in the symbolism of the Sufis. This mystical sect of Islam frequently wrote and sang of their great feasts at which they ate and drank immoderately. An example of their symbolism is the rubaiyat of Omar Khayyam. But the Sufis were in reality most sober men and their feasts were of the spirit, not the body. Their wine was the spirit of God and their food was wisdom. They sat together feasting upon the mystery of life.

THE RAISING OF LAZARUS

According to the Gospels, Jesus performed the miracle of raising the dead on three occasions. He awakened the daughter of the priest of the Sanhedrin; he raised up the man of Nain; and he resurrected Lazarus from the tomb. There is a certain progression in the power of these miracles. The daughter of the elder had just died; the young man of Nain was raised as his body was being taken to the grave; and Lazarus was resurrected after four days being dead in the tomb.

Certain modern secret societies which have descended from the ancient Egyptian Mysteries preserve to this day a symbolic ritual of death and resurrection. In the ancient Mysteries, resurrection signified not the raising of the physical body from physical death, but rather the elevation of the soul or spiritual part from the tomb of the material nature. This resurrection was achieved through the imparting of certain sacred knowledge concerning the origin of the universe and man, and the place of the human soul in the sphere of creation. Plato, an initiate of the Grecian and Egyptian Mysteries, wrote that the body was the sepulcher of the soul. In another place he amplifies this statement when he says that the body of man conceals within it a spiritual nature in the same way that the shell of an oyster contains within it the living organism.

Philosophically speaking, therefore, resurrection must mean the higher or immortal part of man rising out of ignorance, materiality, and corruption. It was for this reason that the hermetic adepts were called twice-born, for they had received a new life in Truth. Such is the true meaning of the Scriptural verse, John 3:3: "Jesus answered and said unto him, Verily, verily, I say unto thee, Except a man be born again, he cannot see the kingdom of God." Nicodemus asked if a man could a second time enter into his mother's womb to be born. Jesus answered John 3:6: "That which is born of the flesh is flesh; and that which is born of the Spirit is spirit." This statement is in perfect harmony and accord with the old pagan rites. A man born of the flesh is mortal, but if that man be born again in the spirit through wisdom and initiation, he is immortal.

The account of the raising of the daughter of Jairus is given in the 8th chapter of Luke. Jesus came into the house of Jairus and taking the hand of the daughter of Jairus who lay dead, he called to her, saying, "Maid, arise." The spirit returned to her body and she arose from the couch of death, Jesus commanded that she be given food.

In Luke 7:11-15 is described the raising of the widow's son. At the gate of the city of Nain, Jesus and his disciples beheld a dead man being carried out. The youth's mother who was a widow was weeping. Jesus had compassion on her and he said to the dead man: "Young man, I say unto thee, Arise." Thereupon the young man that was dead arose and spoke.

The account of the raising of Lazarus is in John 11. When Jesus came to Bethany, he found that Lazarus had been buried in the tomb for four days. He went to the tomb and ordered that the stone should be rolled away. He then Cried with a loud voice: "Lazarus, come forth." John 11:44 reads; "And he that was dead came forth, bound hand and foot with grave-clothes: and his face was bound about with a napkin. Jesus said unto them, Loose him, and let him go."

Jesus gave certain instructions to his disciples that they should go forth to teach the Gospel, heal the sick, raise the dead, cast out demons, and cleanse the lepers. Each of these injunctions has a definite, symbolic meaning. To preach the Gospel meant to teach or inform those who were prepared to receive instruction. To heal the sick was to remedy not merely the infirmities of the flesh, but those of ignorance, fear, and superstition. To raise the dead meant to recover souls from materiality by the word of Truth. To cast out demons meant to modify the passions, emotions, and appetites. And to cleanse the lepers meant to purify those who were unclean of thought and deed. All this regeneration takes place within the individual himself when he has received the Law into his own nature and soul. Jesus, the personification of wisdom, says in John 11:25: "I am the resurrection, and the life; he that believeth in me, though he were dead, yet shall he live."

The Platonic theology describes the state of unenlightened man as sleep. Though he lives in the material world, yet he sleeps, because his reason is not awakened and he wanders as a dreamer in a world of reality, even as the wise man stands as a reality in a world of dreams. Such was the state of the daughter of Jairus. The man of Nain, the son of the widow, a symbol carried over from the Egyptian rites of Osiris, is more completely dead, the body having been prepared for burial. Materiality and illusion have dominated the purposes of life; the soul is obscured and defeated by its material part so that it is truly ready for the oblivion of the tomb. Lazarus has lain for four days in the sepulcher of the vault. Even his flesh has rotted; in other words, corruption has dominated his life.

Yet in each of these three cases, the power of Truth makes the body whole. He who sleeps, he who is dead, and he who is buried, all are brought back to life, life here representing a condition of spiritual awareness. We are dealing with no literal resurrection of the flesh, but with a mystery, the mystery of internal resurrection through initiation into the Mysteries. In these Mysteries, Jesus stands as the hierophant, and into his mouth are placed the words of the high priest. He is made a personification of the Truth which he represents.

There is another interpretation by which it is revealed that these three who were dead were initiated into his sect by being lifted from a material state to a condition of participation in the arcana or secret doctrine. In certain secret orders, it is preserved to this day that the neophyte is regarded as one dead, and that he is brought to life by the Master of the Temple. By this it is inferred that life is consciousness and wisdom, and those who do not possess it are dead though they seem to live. He who possesses the Truth shall still live though he seems to die. Wisdom bestows immortality upon internal consciousness. Immortality is not continuance in one body, but the continuance of consciousness through many bodies. All of this is magnificently revealed in the Mysteries of Egypt and Greece.

THE MIRACULOUS DRAUGHT OF FISHES

In Luke 5:4-10 it is told that Jesus went into a ship and bade Simon to launch out into the deep and let down his nets. Simon answered that they had toiled all the night and had taken nothing. But he obeyed the instruction. When they had let down their nets, the draught was so great that the nets broke and the fishermen had to call for help. After this miracle Iames, John, and Simon followed after him and become his disciples.

Jesus said: "From henceforth, thou shalt catch men." The sea is the symbol of the illusional universe, the sphere of doubt and uncertainty, for even as the sea is moved by every wind, so the uncertain man is moved by every doubt. In India, the sea is maya, illusion, the symbol of the temporal universe and all that it contains, ruled over by leering Yama, the god of misery and pain. Those who love the truth are indeed fishers of men, for they cast their nets into the sea and the nets are filled with souls. The fish is one of the most ancient symbols of the human soul, and it was the original symbol of Christianity.

Jesus as the personification of Truth is the fisher of men. Jesus as the fisher of men, or the fish man, appears to come from the Chaldean story of Dagon who came out of the sea and brought religion, philosophy, and science to his people. In the Bible there is Esdras, the man who came from the sea. The New Testament makes several uses of the fish symbolism. There is the coin in the fish's mouth, and the feeding of the multitude with the two fishes and the barley loaves. St. Augustine said that Christ was a fish broiled and eaten by sinners for their redemption.

The death and resurrection of Christ is said to be prefigured by Jonah who remained three days in the belly of a great fish, even as Christ remained three days on the earth. In India, the first avatar of Vishnu is in the form of a fish swimming in the great ocean of space. The symbolism appears to be as follows: There are two seas—that which is below the firmament, called the sea of illusion in which dwell men represented as small fishes swimming in its depths; and that which is above the firmament, the Schamayim, the sea of the waters of life in which abides the great fish which, like the serpent of Aaron, eats up all the small fishes.

In the Brahmanic account of the flood, the Hindu Noah enters his ark and casts a rope from the bow. Vishnu in the form of a great fish then draws the ark; safely through the deluge. In the Hebrew account, there is a great creature too vast to be allowed in the ark which swims alongside and directs the course. The account is not in the Bible but in the apocryphal commentaries. When the vernal equinox occurred in Pisces, the fishes, it was taught that the Messiah, the sun god, took upon himself the form of a fish—that is, the sun annually was born at the vernal equinox through a fish's body, the sign of Pisces. The redeemer god always assumes the form of the sign ascending at the vernal equinox. Thus, in the age of Pisces he takes the form of a fish. In the previous cycle, he took the form of the lamb or ram, the scapegoat of Israel, and Jupiter-Ammon. Prior to this, the sun god took the form of the bull, Apis and the golden calf.

Thus, astronomy plays an important part in Biblical symbolism. The Christian dispensation occurred near the end of the cycle of the ram and close to the beginning of the cycle of the fish. Jesus refers to himself as the alpha and the omega, the first and the last, the beginning and the end: The first sign of the zodiac is Aries, the ram, and the last sign is Pisces, the fishes. Therefore, Jesus is truly the lamb of God and the fisher of men. The lamb and the fish were the only Christian symbols known to the early church.

THE LORD'S PRAYER

The Lord's prayer as given in Matt. 6:9-13 is generally believed to be a unique document of supreme Christian significance. In fact, the Lord's prayer is derived in its entirety from the Talmud and is an old Jewish prayer somewhat abridged. The original prayer reads:

"Our father which art in heaven, be gracious to us, O Lord, our God; hallowed be thy name, and let the remembrance of thee be glorified in heaven above, and upon the earth here below. Let thy kingdom reign over us, now and forever. Thy holy men of old saith, Remit and forgive unto ALL MEN WHATSOEVER THEY HAVE DONE against me. And lead us not into temptation, but DELIVER US FROM the EVIL thing. For THINE is the kingdom, and thou shalt reign in glory, forever and forevermore."

Certain of the changes which now appear in the King James version are translational rather than factual. If these errors were corrected the Lord's prayer would resemble even more closely this old version.

There is a deep cabalistical significance to this prayer which is susceptible of division into ten parts, corresponding to the ten names of God in the Cabala. Like the ten commandments, it corresponds to the ten blossoms on the sephirothic tree, beginning with our Father which is Kether the crown, and ending with Malchuth which means the kingdom, the tenth or inferior part of the universe. The esoteric significance of this prayer has been entirely lost to the modern Christian world and it has deteriorated into a mere formula of words frequently recited without any conception of the mysteries which it contains.

The sephirothic tree with its ten ineffable blossoms represents the ten parts of the universe. The first three sephiroth or flowers are the three powers of the godhead, and the other seven are the planets of which the moon is the lowest. This reveals that the ancient Jews were aware of the esoteric fact that the material universe is not one of the divine principles but rather a negative field in which these principles operate. Therefore, the prayer cabalistically adores the three greater and seven lesser powers in which we live, move, and have our being, and of whose natures we are compounded.

In Math. 6:7 Jesus is made to say: "But when ye pray use not vain repetitions, as the heathens do; for they think that they shall be heard for their much speaking." Unfortunately, the greater part of Christendom has fallen into vain repetition. In Matt. 6:6 is the admonition: "But thou, when thou prayest, enter into thy closet, and when thou hast shut thy door, pray to thy Father which is in secret." It would be vain to believe that the merit of prayer would be increased by going into a small room and closing the door. The inner meaning of the symbolism is that he who would pray should enter into his own inner consciousness, the closet symbolizing the heart, and when he has shut the door, that is closed off external interference, he should pray to his father which is in secret. According to the old mysteries, the secret father, or as the Greeks called it, the hidden god, abode in, the heart, that is in the sanctum sanctorum. Man prays not to some vast spirit in the sky, but rather to the divine principle within himself, that is his god, his own spirit, his own over-self, the father that abides in the innermost. Many have raised their eyes to the skies, but few have turned them inward to the contemplation of the hidden god.

In verse 22 of the same chapter is a most occult secret: "The light of the body is the eye; if therefore thine eye be single, thy-whole body shall be full of light." The eye single, the third eye painted on the foreheads of oriental gods, the inner eye, the symbolic eye of Horus, sees inwardly whereas the physical eyes behold only the outer parts. It is with the eye single, the eye of the gods, that man can behold the sanctum sanctorum, the little room in the heart, where between the wings of the cherub hovers the shekinah's glory.

In the eddas is described the descent of Odin to the roots of the Yggdrasill Tree where lays the cool, smooth surface of Mimir's pool. Odin spoke to Mimir, the god of memory and wisdom, and begged the knowledge of all things, and Mimir spoke and said: "If thou wouldst know things, pluck out thy eye and cast it into my pool." Odin did so, and received the knowledge of every mystery except the secret of his own death. Here is another statement of the same mystical truth. It's also taught in the Hebrew tradition that the great universal man whose body is the universe has likewise but one eye with neither eyelid nor eyelash, for it is written that: "The god of Israel neither slumbers nor sleeps."

The significance of prayer has been hopelessly distorted by the decadence and corruption of our theologies. Philosophically speaking, prayer is a statement of reality, it is not a constant begging for the things of this world. Even in the Lord's prayer, there is a double meaning to each of the parts by which a mysticism is revealed to the enlightened but concealed from the profane. The parts of the prayer with their interpretations are as follows:

Our Father which art in Heaven.

By Father is to be understood the source of ourselves, not a person but a principle, the divine life from which we have been individualized by the processes of evolution. Which art in heaven means that this divine principle abides in the sphere of causes, heaven, or the higher part of the universal creation. Heaven is not a place, but a refinement of matter, a higher degree of vibration. Therefore, to paraphrase we may say, our cause which is ever in the spiritual part of the universe.

Hallowed be thy name.

Hallowed meaning venerated or revered and name being the symbol by which we denominate that which is beyond comprehension or estimation. All together meaning we venerate first cause through its name or manifestation.

Thy kingdom come.

By the kingdom of heaven is meant a general spiritual state or a condition of enlightenment or participation in truth, that is may the divine be made manifest.

Thy will be done in earth as it is in heaven.

By will we shall understand law and the divine plan which must be manifested on earth through the initiated or the enlightened and by a spiritualizing of all institutions. As it is in heaven infers that in the spiritual world, the will of first cause perfectly administers all things according to its own purpose. In substance, the divine law shall be made manifest in earthly things as it is evident in all cosmic things.

Give us this day our daily bread.

We should remember that bread does not necessarily mean food, for it is stated in the Gospel that Christ himself was the bread which came down from heaven. Consequently, this does not imply that it is the duty of First Cause to supply all men with material abundance. Rather let us this day realize that part of truth which is necessary to our daily virtue.

And forgive us our debts, as we forgive our debtors.

Debts in this case refer to our universal indebtedness and the errors by which we have deviated from the divine plan. And by forgive we should understand a full acceptance of responsibility and the correction of error through right action. In other words, in our imperfection and ignorance we are constantly breaking universal law. Let us be given the wisdom and the strength to correct our errors.

And lead us not into temptation.

This is one of the most difficult verses to interpret for the reason that it is inconceivable that a divine benevolence should ever be responsible for encouraging delinquency. The error is due to the old form which has never been correctly translated. The true thought means that in the workings of universal law of which we are all hopelessly ignorant, we may go astray, and we beg that our lower animal nature shall not lead us from the path of righteousness. It is the old problem of the willingness of the spirit but the weakness of the flesh. We are addressing this verse to that hierarchy of the divine order that is particularly concerned with the emotional existence of man.

But deliver us from evil.

Here again we are not actually asking God to save us but rather we are addressing the human mind and the mind of the universe which through reason and truth will finally bring us into the perfect participation with good.

The final part is an encomium. The kingdom the power and the glory are the three persons of the triad. Power the first person, glory the second, and the kingdom the third. The word amen is from Ammon the father god of Egypt and was an ancient Egyptian salutation to the supreme power of the universe.

Sincerely yours,
Manly P. Hall

LETTER NO. 9

Dear Friend,

THE SECRET DOCTRINE IN THE BIBLE

There is abundant evidence that the early Christian church fraternized with the pagan systems of its day. It is only in more recent times that ecclesiastics have hurled their anathemas at nonconformists. The Emperor

Hadrian writing to his brother-in-law Servianus, says: "Those who worship Serapis are likewise Christians; even those who style themselves the bishops of Christ are devoted to Serapis. The very patriarch himself, when he comes to Egypt, is forced by some to adore Serapis, by others to worship Christ. There is but one God to them all. Him do the Christians, him do the Jews, him do the Gentiles, all alike worship."

Severus Alexander, another Roman Emperor, daily paid his devotion to Christ and Abraham, and at the same time spent huge sums of money decorating the temples of Serapis and Isis "with statues, couches, and all things pertaining to their mysteries." From these statements it is obvious that the founders of the Christian faith had a religious tolerance entirely beyond the comprehension of their modern successors.

JESUS WALKING ON THE WATER

The miracle of Jesus walking on the water is to be found in John 6:19-20. His disciples had entered a ship to reach Capernaum. Jesus was not with them. A great wind arose which threatened the ship, and in the midst of the storm they saw Jesus walking towards them on the sea. They were greatly terrified. "But he said unto them, It is I, be not afraid."

By the troubled sea we are to understand life with its storms and trials. In the midst of the sea, the little ship of disciples represents humanity. The ship is in danger of foundering and the disciples are afraid. Then in the midst of the sea, walking peacefully upon the waters, appears the form of Jesus, the symbol of Truth that quiets the sea of life. When peace and wisdom are in the heart of man, the sea can no longer be troubled. There are no more storms and man himself, like Peter when he held his faith, can walk likewise upon the waters.

There are many accounts in the religions of the world of gods, priests, and heroes who walked upon the waters. In every case the meaning is the same. It is faith quieting the storms of life. It is wisdom waling safely over the illusion. In one of the Eastern myths or legends, it is written that the great Buddhist sage Bodhidharma walked across the China Sea on a leaf. There is also the story of the old Buddhist monk who walked along the shore.

In his meditation, while contemplating the reality and ignoring his surroundings, he came to the end of the path and walked right out onto the ocean. Suddenly awakening from his meditation and looking around him in amazement, fear came. Straightway he sank and nearly drowned. In the early Mysteries of the Druids, part of the initiation consisted of drifting out into the open sea in a small boat without oars. Only those who could control the elements by their own will could return alive. The successful neophyte appeared in the midst of the storm standing in his little boat, the waves opened on each side of him, and he rode peacefully to the shore as a sign that his fitness for initiation in the secret rites had been proved.

All of these are symbolic stories. The sea represents emotion. Only those who master emotion are capable of illumination. The Master walking on the water represents the higher nature of each man, firm and courageous, quelling the tempest of life. This is one of the noblest and most inspiring of the biblical allegories.

THE LAST SUPPER

The most complete account of the Last Supper and the words attributed to Jesus on this occasion are to be found in John 13 to 17 inclusive. Additional details are to be found in Luke 22. During the Last Supper Christ as a "priest after the order of Melchizedek," performs the Eucharistic ceremony of the communion of bread and wine.

In the Dionysiac rites of the Greeks, the god himself represented life in its two primary aspects—spiritual and physical. The spiritual was inspirational; the physical, nutritional—these mysteries represented by wine and bread. The Greeks claimed that by the blood of the god was to be understood the light of the spirit, or a participation in spiritual ecstasy; and by the body of the god, physical sustenance. There is a great mystery concealed in this symbolism, the mystery of the god whose blood is life, and whose body is the world. The Christian sacrament of communion seems to have received great inspiration from these Bacchic rites.

We have abundant records that the early rituals of the Bacchanalia were accompanied by music and song, and frequently the dance. The early fathers of the church—Tertullian, Cyril, and St. Augustine—have preserved evidence that the Master and his disciples sang together at the Last Supper, and according to at least one account, they danced together. The song has been preserved for us and is as follows:

I wish to unbind, and I wish to be unbound.

I wish to save, and I wish to be saved.

I wish to beget, and I wish to be begotten.

I wish to sing; dance ye all with joy.

I wish to weep; be ye all struck with grief.

I wish to adorn, and l wish to be adorned.

I am the lamp for you who see me.

I am the gate for you who knock.

Ye who see what I do, do not tell what I am doing.

I have enacted all in this discourse.

And I have not been in any way deceived.

Many Bible students are not aware that certain quotations attributed to Jesus have survived that are not to be found in the gospels. This is proved by a statement in Acts 20:35: "Remember the words of the Lord Jesus, how he said, "It is more blessed to give than to receive." According to St. Clement, Christ was asked upon one occasion when his kingdom would be established upon the earth, and Christ answered: "It will only come when two and two make one, when the outside resembles the inside, and when there is neither male nor female."

St. Ignatius in his epistle to the Smyrnaeans amplifies the text of Luke 24:39. The King James version reads: "Handle me, and see; for a spirit hath not flesh and bones, as ye see me have."

St. Ignatius makes Christ say: "Take hold on me, and touch me, and see that I am not an incorporeal demon."

The astronomical implication of the last supper is evident. In the first century of the Christian era, the vernal equinox occurred in the sign of the ram, that is the sun was annually born in that sign. For this reason, Christ is called the Lamb of God. His picture with the lamb in his arms, on the walls of the Roman catacombs, is referred to as the Good Shepherd in ecclesiastical literature, and was originally symbolized by the Christian bishops as the Agnus Dei, the Lamb of God slain for the sins of the world. Seated in the midst of his disciples, the Messiah is therefore the sun-god, in the midst of the zodiac, the twelve signs of which have long been attributed to these disciples. For example, Matthew, Mark, Luke and John are associated with the four creatures, the lion, the bull, the man, and the eagle, and are so represented on early Christian sarcophagi. The analogy between the disciples and the zodiac was derived from the Latins and Greeks who distributed their twelve principal gods among the twelve zodiacal constellations.

The Passover is the annual passing over of the sun from the southern to the northern hemispheres according to primitive ideas concerning astronomy. The sacrifice of the lamb at this period was practiced by the pagan Greeks who regarded the vernal equinox as the annual rebirth of the savior god. The ceremony of Easter is the perpetuation of pagan equinoctial rites.

The place of Judas Iscariot in this mystery drama has never been clearly set forth. The word Iscariot means a man of cities, but this does not clarify the problem to any great degree. Judas betrayed his Lord for thirty pieces of silver, but a clue to the facts is to be discovered by carefully comparing the various accounts of Judas contained in the New Testament books. In Luke 17:12, Judas is called the "son of perdition." In John 13:27, it is written "Satan entered into him." In Matthew 27:5, Judas after betraying Christ "cast down the pieces of silver in the temple, and departed, and went and hanged himself." Acts 1:25 tells us: "Judas by transgression fell, that he might go to his own place." Acts 1:18 states that Judas "purchased a field with the reward of iniquity," it further adds that he died as a result of a fall.

To these somewhat contradictory remarks we learn that the gospel writers were not very sure what did happen to Judas. It appears that Judas is the Egyptian Typhon, Job's Satan, and Scandinavia's Loki. He is the personification of the adversary. He is introduced into the drama as a symbol of the intrinsic imperfection of all living things. In the zodiac he is Scorpio by some calculations; and by others, Capricorn. He is the backbiter, the destroyer. He is still preserved in the church as the "devil's advocate."

If the gods gathered in any place or time, Satan was also with them. In the Christian mysteries, the disciples were the members of Christ, just as the various zodiacal signs are distributed over the curious figure in the almanac. This figure represents the world or the universe, and to the ancients, the zodiac revealed through its twelve parts the twelve members of the world. Of this twelve-fold body, one part is traitor to the rest.

Boehme calls this traitor the "will of the abyss" or the "relapsed Adam." He also refers to it as "self-will," that is the ego complex in man. This ego complex is the center or nucleus of selfishness, self-purpose, and self-mind. This is the traitor, the slayer of the real. To express it more simply, we each have a personal will rooted in the complex of selfness or "I am." Judas is disappointed and embittered because Jesus was not going to become a physical king over the Jews; that is, that the Divine Purpose was not going to achieve a personal advantage. Therefore, self-will revolts against Divine Will, the personal betrays the universal. This is the life of every man, for thus betrayed the universal is doomed to die upon the cross of matter. It is truth sacrificed to personal advantage. Judas would exploit wisdom. Judas is the exploiter, whereas Christ represents Universal Will and Universal Purpose. In every man there is a struggle between the universal and the personal, therefore, it is said of Judas that Satan entered into him. Satan is the old serpent who tempted primitive man to egoism through the famous apple allegory in the Garden of Eden.

Judas is called the man of the cities because egoism is a symbol of temporal power and a desire for temporal power. First, Satan tempts Jesus from the mountain top, promising him the cities of the earth; that is, man is tempted to sacrifice his spiritual advantages for material purposes. Then Satan enters into Judas whose name means cities and causes his betrayal. The thirty pieces of silver represent the material advantages for which Judas betrayed his Lord. The money is finally used however to buy a potter's field to bury the nameless dead, thus completing and rounding out the allegory, and providing ample inference for the interpretation.

THE GARDEN OF GETHSEMANE

Matt. 26:36-57 describe the ordeal of Gethsemane. In no part of the New Testament is it more clearly indicated that Jesus did not regard himself as identical with God the Father. The identity of the three persons of the Trinity was determined by a series of church councils which had little regard for the letter of the gospels. The prayer of Jesus in Gethsemane is given in Matt. 26:39: "O, my Father, if it be possible, let this cup pass from me: nevertheless, not as I will, but as thou wilt." From these words it is clearly revealed that Jesus did not possess power over the Father, or power with the Father, but rather besought the Father for mercy. Here also Jesus resists his destiny, but, finally, acknowledges the supremacy of the Father's will. Matt. 26:42: "O, my Father, if this cup may not pass away from me, except I drink it, thy will be done."

According to the old doctrines of the Gnostics, Jesus was over-shadowed by the Messias or Sotar. When the ministry was finished, the Sotar retired into the higher Aeon's and left Jesus to suffer and die alone. They give us this as the true interpretation of the words of Jesus upon the cross: "My God, my God, why hast thou forsaken me." Matt. 27:46.

Mohammed whose contact with Christianity was through Nestorian monks in the Arabian deserts had definite opinions on the fate of Jesus. "They devised a stratagem against him, but God devised a stratagem against them, and God is the best deviser of stratagems." In another place the Prophet of Islam says: "The malice of his (Jesus) enemies aspersed his reputation, and conspired against his life, but their intention only was guilty—a phantom or criminal was substituted on the cross, and the innocent Jesus was translated into the seventh heaven." Koran 153, v. 53, and 104, v. 156.

The Egyptian Basilides, a disciple of Matthias, says that Peter told him that Cerinthus was crucified in the place of Christ, that Christ himself did not die, but ascended to the higher Aeon's.

It is evident that the last days of Jesus are a great mystery. The Manichaeans and other initiated sects of the Near East insist that a sublime secret is concealed within the account of the passion. Indeed, as St. Paul has said, the crucifixion is a stumbling block. Paul could not know that this stumbling block would remain to the twentieth century.

CHRIST BEFORE PILATE

The earliest reference to Jesus in secular history occurs in Pliny's famous letter to Trajan, and in the annals of Tacitus, both works belonging to the second century A.D. Our present descriptions of Jesus are derived principally from works attributed to Pontius Pilate and Publius Lentulus. Both of these descriptions are regarded as comparatively late forgeries, probably originating between the 11th and 14th centuries. Pontius Pilate appears to have been the procurator of Judea from A.D. 27 to A.D. 37. The Roman officials kept a complete record of the various cases which appeared before them. There is no entry that can be regarded as coinciding with the account given in the gospels. The Roman law in Judea was very exact in the matter of penalties for various crimes and misdemeanors. Crucifixion was reserved for crimes of great physical violence such as highway robbery and murder. The penalties for civil offenses and religious misdemeanors was death by stoning or the sword.

In the Archiepiscopal Palace at Bourges was long preserved the pretended order for the execution of Jesus. It read as follows: "Jesus of Nazareth, of the Jewish tribe of Juda, convicted of imposture and rebellion against the divine authorities of Tiberius Augustus, Emperor of the Romans, having for this sacrilege been condemned to die on the cross by sentence of the judge, Pontius Pilate, on the prosecution of our lord Herod, lieutenant of the Emperor of Judaea shall be taken tomorrow morning, the 23rd day of the Ides of March, to the usual place of punishment, under the escort of a company of the Praetorian Guard. The so-called King of the Jews shall be taken out by the Strumean Gate. All the public officers and the subjects of the Emperor are directed to lend their aid to the execution of this sentence. "(Signed) CAPEL. Jerusalem, the 23rd day of the Ides of March, year of Rome, 783."

According to this document the crucifixion occurred in A.D. 30. If, as Eusebius states, the ministry of Jesus lasted nearly 4 years, the ministry began A.D. 26. All of this is very confusing and leads to the inevitable conclusion that the entire subject has been obscured by misunderstanding and imposture. There is also great controversy over the character of Pilate.

According to Philo and Josephus, Pilate was a man of violent and obstinate disposition who terrorized the countryside and sought above all other things to destroy the laws and privileges of the Jews. He promoted civil strife, his spies were constantly bringing in reports of treason, and he was in every way contrary to the Pilate of the gospels, who is depicted as a gentle soul of compassionate nature who washed his hands of the entire matter.

In metaphysical symbolism, Christ before Pilate signifies the conflict between spiritual and temporal power. It signifies also that the temporal has dominion over the spiritual in the physical world, but that the spiritual rises triumphantly over the material in the superphysical world. Strangely enough, Pilate sees no wrong in the man and returns him to the Jews. That is, Jesus is finally condemned by ecclesiastical law. This is strangely reminiscent of religion as a whole. It is not the materialist but the theologian who destroys his own faith.

CRUCIFIXION

There is a rare manuscript of the apostle Barnabas which was for some time in the possession of Cranmer in which it is definitely stated that Christ was not crucified. He was carried into the third heaven by the four angels, Gabriel, Michael, Raphael, and Uriel. Judas died in his place.

It is impossible at this late time to determine with certainty how much of the gospel story is to be accepted literally, and how much is to be understood as a mystery "in the Spirit." We must remind all sincere Bible students of the words of Synesius, Bishop of Alexandria: "Therefore, as a bishop of the church, I will continue to disseminate the fables of the church, but in my private capacity I shall remain a philosopher to the end."

It was the honest conviction of the Patristic Fathers that the deeper mysteries of the Christian dispensation were beyond the understanding of the laity. In order, therefore, not to "cast pearls before swine," they devised a cycle of fables which have come to be accepted as literal historical facts. From various causes the same general condition has arisen in most religions. Spiritual matters can not be understood by those not spiritually enlightened. Again, enlightenment can not be bestowed; it must be evolved. To be serviceable, a religion must be comprehensible to the mass of its followers. The result is inevitably a compromise with truth. In serving the uninformed many, theology leaves the enlightened few without adequate spiritual food.

Jacobus de Voragine in his golden legend compiled the extravagant legends of medieval theology. His monumental work loaded with absurdity and superstition became a textbook for the pious who doubted not one jot or tittle of it. It is exceedingly difficult critically and yet sympathetically to discover the golden thread of truth in the tangled skeins of tradition. There is no virtue in perpetuating the false, nor is there any virtue in discarding entirely that which may contain vital and significant truth. We must search for meaning, but we must not manufacture meaning. We may desire to discern the mystery, but our desire must not become the parent of false interpretation.

The crucifixion of Christ is the real foundation of Christianity. Christ was the first martyr of the church, and by his death bestowed permanence upon the teachings of his disciples. The crucifixion is the blood of atonement. Theologians insist that the blood of Christ spilled upon Golgotha purifies all who believe on him, and by a unique virtue cleanses all men of original sin. This is, indeed, a strange foundation for a faith and is peculiar to Christendom alone of all great religions. Gradually the cross has come to be regarded as the proper symbol of Christ, and the crucifix a constant reminder of what Christians like to call "the drama of the ages." Yet frankly and honestly, this entire belief and all the consequences that have been built upon it, have been founded on a most insecure foundation. There is no absolute proof the crucifixion did not take place, nor is there any absolute proof that it did take place. The principal and almost sole foundations of the crucifixion account are in the gospels, and the immense literature derived from the gospels. It follows therefore that until the gospels themselves are authenticated and their true authorship determined, no account peculiar to them can be regarded as historically established.

Nor do we desire to be regarded as merely quibbling. Making much out of little. The truth is there is less actually known historically about the founding of Christianity than any other great historical event in the last three thousand years. That the gospels contain at least mistaken information is now proved beyond doubt, and it is impossible to state with certainty where such errors end.

For two thousand years the New Testament has been taken on faith, and upon the personal convictions of individuals not in a position to prove what they believe. No one will deny the sincerity and devotion of those hundreds of millions who have accepted Christianity. Nor is it of great spiritual significance whether their belief is based upon fact or fable if they have lived well and have been induced into courses of tolerance, honesty, gentleness, and wisdom. All other factors are of secondary importance.

Where history impinges upon the moral life, however, has been in the matter of tolerance. It is the tolerance aspect which makes facts necessary. I think most will agree that the Christian church has not had a distinguished record for tolerance. Intolerance is based upon a small certainty about things unknown. Yet intolerance can be the destroyer of religions and nations, hence the necessity for the statement of doubt and the moderation of theological enthusiasm.

An examination of the crucifixion from a philosophical standpoint inclines the mind towards the belief the account is allegorical rather than literal. At least the significance is allegorical. The crucifixion myth occurs too frequently in the history of ancient religions. We become convinced that it has some esoteric significance. We are certainly spiritually enriched by such a conclusion. We transform history into living fact when we perceive eternal truths shadowed forth through presumably historical circumstances.

The crucifixion is believed to have taken place on a small hill outside of Jerusalem, now called Gordon's Calvary. The rock formations on the side of the hill cause it to resemble a great skull, thus explaining the name of Calvary or Golgotha, both of which refer to a skull. Jerusalem is what is called a walking city, that is, it gradually has changed location over a long period of time. Its present boundaries were not those of two thousand years ago. According to the Roman church, the original site of Calvary is enclosed within the area of the Church of the Holy Sepulcher. The presumed location of the original cross is marked by a gold ornament set in the floor. A short distance off on each side are two other inlays, one of black and one of white. These mark the places where stood the crosses of the two thieves, the white inlay signifying the repentant thief.

According to the gospel account, Jesus was crucified directly over the burial place of Adam. This is mystically set forth on certain crucifixes by the addition of small skull and crossbones near the foot of the cross. After Noah had removed the body of Adam from the ark, buried it on Golgotha. Accounts like this contribute to the realization that we are dealing with spiritual allegories rather than historical facts.

Christ was fastened to the cross by three nails, the feet being crossed. The cabalists explain that the fourth nail of the crucifixion was stolen by a magician. The three remaining nails survive in symbolism to this day as the British mark of the broad arrows. There has been a definite schism in the Christian church over the problem of whether or not there should be three or four nails.

The crucifixion depicts the Messiah, the guiltless one, dying between two thieves who were not nailed to their crosses but were tied thereon by ropes. When the mother of Constantine claimed to have found the true cross with its nails, the Emperor Constantine used one of them as a bit for his horse. A second nail is believed to have been melted into the crown of Hungary, the famous "iron crown." This is most extraordinary inasmuch as nails were not known in Syria at that time, and if spikes of any kind were used, they must have been wooden pegs.

Why is the crucifixion present in more than a dozen ancient religions? Why was Prometheus crucified on Mt. Caucasus with a vulture gnawing at his liver? And Christ on Mt. Calvary with the Spear of Longinus thrust into his right side? Prometheus brought the fire of God, wisdom, to men. Christ brought "light that lighteth every man that cometh into the world." The mystery is explained when we understand the words attributed to St. Paul: "Christ in you, the hope of glory."

In the mystical theosophy of the Gnostics and other early Christian sects, it was taught that mind consisted of two parts by nature called by the Platonists intelligible and intellectual, and by modern philosophers abstract and concrete thought. The Orientals teach that the two parts of the mind are symbolized by the two lobes of the brain. Abstract and concrete mind are the two thieves, Gestas and Demas. Christ as pure knowledge or Truth is, therefore, represented as crucified in equilibrium between the two extremities of thought. This further points to the teaching of Pythagoras that virtue is always in moderation or in a middle distance between extremes. The lower mind does not repent, but the higher mind becoming aware of Truth is promised by the Messiah that it shall be with him in paradise.

The natural function of mind is the estimation of phenomena. The mind looking outwardly through the brain observes and contemplates the mysteries of the physical universe, or of the body. The lower mind is the instrument of habit, appetite, emotion, sensation, and self-preservation. The higher mind accepts to itself philosophy, religion, and the arts, and contemplates the more refined elements of material existence. It is this higher mind which by discipline can be lifted up into a recognition of Divine Truth. Mind can never grasp Reality, but it can recognize dimly the significance of Reality. Truth can never be reduced to thought, but thought may contemplate Truth from afar, honoring even though understanding is impossible.

If by Christ, then, we represent Truth which is the first-born of Reality, the eternal Messiah, the universal Savior, we have perceived the substance behind the shadow. As long as we are satisfied with a merely literal explanation, pinning our hope of salvation upon the historical circumstance, we have not gone far in the understanding of spiritual mysteries.

Truth manifesting the material universe is hopelessly obscured by the inadequate vehicles of its manifestation. Perfection manifesting through the imperfect appears by very necessity to be imperfect itself. Wisdom is exploited into scheming; thought is misused; the energies of life are dissipated; and the Divine Plan is indeed crucified in man and in nature. The finest part of life is reduced to servitude to the material and man, a son of the Infinite, dedicates himself only to the finite. Yet this truth which is crushed to earth in the life of each person does not utterly die. Like a seed planted in the earth, it remains dead until aspiration brings it to life. The true resurrection is the lifting up of Truth in the individual; the resurrection of the eternal in the temporal; the resurrection of virtue always latent in man. This latent power manifests forth in all its glory when study and experience have released the individual from bondage to appetite and desire.

THE EMPTY TOMB

In the 20th chapter of John is described the visit of Mary Magdalene to the tomb of Jesus. Joseph of Arimathea besought Pilate that he might take the body of Jesus and prepare it for burial. It was this same Joseph, according to the Glastonbury legend, who later travelled across Europe bearing with him the wreath of thorns. Reaching England, Joseph of Arimathea built the Abbey of Glastonbury and planted the wreath of thorns which took root and became the celebrated Glastonbury thorns. He is believed also to have carried with him the Holy Grail, and in the past years several excavations have been carried on at Glastonbury in the hope that the cup might be rediscovered.

According to the gospel account, Mary Magdalene found the tomb empty and the great stone rolled away. From this occurrence the story of the Holy Sepulcher had its origin. The supposed tomb of Christ now stands in the center of a great rotunda in the Church of the Holy Sepulcher in Jerusalem. The tomb itself is a small cube-like room ornately decorated with the tributes of fifteen centuries. The sarcophagus itself runs along one wall of the crypt resembling a low stone bench. In the middle of the crypt is the stone upon which the angel sat—at least, so the guides tell us.

For centuries, the Holy Sepulcher was in the hands of Islam and Christians were forbidden the right of pilgrimage. The result was the crusades in which the knights and nobles of the kingdoms and principalities of Europe went forth against the Saracens to wrest the tomb of the Lord from the hands of the infidel.

The truth of the matter was that Europe was gradually emerging from a feuded state to national existence. Feudal lords and robber barons fought against the nationalization of countries. Therefore, by a cunningly devised stratagem, these lusty warriors were induced to undertake crusades in Palestine. Many of them died at the siege of Acre; sickness and time took the lives of others; and those who did return discovered that during their absence, their powers and privileges had been removed and Europe had emerged from feudalism into the beginnings of constitutional governments.

In Freemasonry, the Knights Templars or York Rite are still defenders of the Holy Sepulcher. But the literalism of the medieval world has passed. Mysticism has given a new meaning to the old quest. It is now realized that the Holy Sepulcher is not truly in Jerusalem but is the very body of man himself. It is within this body which Plato calls the "sepulcher of the soul" that the divine man lies buried. It is also from this mortal fabric as from a tomb that the immortal man rises up and releases itself as in the mystery of the resurrection. It is now the duty of each man to roll away the stone, that is, to illuminate himself, to rescue his own higher nature from bondage to animal appetites and desire.

The resurrection myth is common to all great religious systems. It is an essential part of religious idealism and derives its authority from the highest and most sublime initiation rituals of Greece, India, and Egypt.

The crusades served a most valuable purpose in addition to disrupting the feudal system. Europe became, for the first time, aware that civilization extended beyond the boundaries of Christendom.

The returning knights described the glory and honor of the Saracen. They had found Islam not a fire-belching dragon, but a world of culture, literature, art, and science. They had found Saladin not only the Emperor of the East, but a wise and generous foe. Many of the nobles brought back with them wives from among the Saracens. This fact is preserved in the heraldry of Europe by the addition of a lunar crescent to the arms of a noble family. With the returning crusaders, science returned to Europe.

So dangerous did this knowledge become to the preferment of European politics, that the Knights Templars were slaughtered, Jacques de Molay burned at the stake, the lands of the Templars confiscated, and themselves accused of practicing heretical rites. But all things work together for good. The search for the Holy Sepulcher resulted in the resurrection of Europe.

Sincerely yours,

Manly P. Hall

LETTER NO. 10

Dear Friend,

THE SECRET DOCTRINE IN THE BIBLE

The resurrection myth is common to most of the great world religions. It seems to have originated among the agricultural folklore of primitive human society. The seed planted in the earth brought forth life. The processes of germination and growth were far beyond the understanding of our agrarian ancestors. The result is a complicated mythology in which hero-gods descend into the earth and finally rise again.

A simple form of the seed myth is to be found in the Babylonian story of Tammuz and Ishtar. Tammuz is the seed that descends into the underworld where it remains as a thing dead until Ishtar, goddess of fertility and the humid vapors of the earth rescues the seed from its dark grave and brings it forth into light.

The resurrection of the seed was not only a mystery in itself, but was intimately associated with human survival. If the seed failed to grow, there was famine and death. Therefore, it was appropriate to offer prayers and sacrifices to propitiate the harvest. A tenth part was put away for the new planting. This is the origin of tithing which has survived as an integral part of many theological systems. There is abundant evidence that the authors of the gospels were aware of the mystery of the seed. Matt. 13 contains several references to the seed myth. In Luke 8: 10-11 is the following highly significant statement: "Unto you it is given to know the mysteries of the kingdom of God: but to others in parables; that seeing they might not see, and hearing they might not understand. Now the parable is this: The seed is the word of God."

We must remember that it is explicitly stated in the gospel according to John that Jesus Christ is the Word, the only begotten of the Father. According to St. Paul, unless the seed dies it cannot live again. Therefore, it becomes obvious to the studiously minded that the writers of the New Testament intended the agricultural myth to be recognized as one of the keys of the resurrection story.

In the gospel according to Luke, chapter 24, is described the empty sepulcher of Jesus. It is further described that Jesus himself came unto the disciples and conversed with them, but they knew him not.

According to the account given in John 20: 16-17, Jesus appeared to Mary Magdalene who immediately recognized him. When Mary turned to him, Jesus said: "Touch me not; for I am not yet ascended to my father." It would be inferred, therefore, that Jesus appeared not in the flesh, but in the spirit by a mystery.

In the seed myth, the holy sepulcher is the calix or seed pod the same as the Grail and the cup of Gethsemane. When the plant emerges from the seed, its form is changed and therefore is not recognizable to those who knew only its previous state. This allegory also has been successfully used in India and China.

The part of Mary of Magdala is an exceedingly strange and important one in the whole New Testament story. Of course, the name Mary means literally water and is an adaptation of the Hebrew name Miriam. The word Magdala means from the Greeks, a tower, a fortress, a place of strength, a defense or security. Like many Bible names, it is a carefully conceived key to the Bible mysteries, like the Helen of the Greeks, Mary Magdalene symbolizes the moon, the consort of the sun; the principle of humidity, water, mare and a high fortress or place of protection, Mary of Magdala is like the Ishtar of the Babylonians and the Mylitta of the Phrygians. She is the mistress of growing things, the very symbol of the humid principle that brings forth life.

Magdalene's place in the New Testament story has been subject to mutilation and change, but still the original principles are faintly evident. Mary recognizes her Lord, but the others gather with him and perceive him not because of the metamorphosis that has taken place. The story has been philosophized and theologized, but still, it is the agricultural myth.

In the last verses of Luke 24: 51, the ascension is described. "And it came to pass, while he blessed them, he was parted from them, and carried up into heaven." To most Bible students, Jesus was physically and literally raised from the dead, appearing physically and literally to his disciples. A study of the gospel account by no means substantiates this attitude, but implies that both the resurrection and ascension were spiritual mysteries. The Christian awaits his day of liberation when he shall be reborn in Christ, but it seems that he is not informed as to the true nature of this spiritual experience.

During centuries of literalism, it was actually believed that a judgment day would come, and in this last day the tombs of the dead would open, and the quick and the dead would come forth to be judged. Some of the early Christian communities believed this so literally and so intensely that they preserved the bodies of their dead in vats of oil so that the flesh would not corrupt, and the man could come forth in his old body for the final judgment. In the light of our present knowledge, we realize that such beliefs are not only inconsistent with the laws of the physical world, but of religion likewise.

The resurrection is not the raising of the dead from their graveclothes and their tombs, but rather the lifting up into life and light of the spiritual nature which is within man. Truly, it is the Christ in you, the hope of glory, that must be raised up. The resurrection is an internal and eternal mystery. It is regeneration, the release of the spiritual entity from its material sepulcher of body, instinct, and appetite.

The mystic resurrection is accomplished in two ways: spiritually through illumination, the sublimation of appetites, and the purification of desires; physically, the spiritual nature is released through the phenomenon of death. According to the terminology of the classical philosophers, death is the accidental separation of the superior and inferior parts of man. The word accidental is used here in its philosophical sense as the antonym of intentional. Resurrection or release through death is a separation rather than a transmutation, therefore it is not regarded as a spiritual victory. Illumination is the conscious separation during life of the divine from the animal man. It is a conscious resurrection. It is a lifting up through effort and integrity. Therefore, it properly may be termed Intentional.

Plato describes the spiritual part of man as imprisoned within the sepulcher of the flesh as the oyster is imprisoned within its shell. This shell is the holy sepulcher, the tomb of a god. The true resurrection is the lifting of the mind from matter and the life from bondage to physical propensities.

There are two forms of death: the first is the separation of the animal nature from its spiritual part through material accident or disease; the other is the dying out of desires, appetites, and other attributes of the animal nature through discipline and regeneration without the dissolution of bodily harmony. This second kind of death is philosophical and truly religious, and finds its place in the symbolism of all the great world religions. When the body is separated from the soul, there is death. When the soul is separated from the body, there is illumination.

In the early Christian church, when a man took holy orders, he was said to "die out of the world, to enter a new life in spirit." For this reason, he usually changed his name (the symbol of his identity), taking some mystical or religious name to represent this transition from one state to another.

He renounced worldliness, took obligations of detachment from material things, and was as a man apart, sanctified unto God. This is a form of the resurrection, and the physical shadow of the greater mysteries which take place in the consciousness itself. Unfortunately, most men can perceive only the body of the law and attempt to obey its letter. The few who are illuminated, however, perceive the soul of the law and become participants in the spiritual mysteries.

THE PARABLES

The parable is a favorite method of religious instruction and is to be found in most of the sacred writings of the world's great religious systems. A parable is a statement of simple truth which by analogy or symbolical extension reveals a greater and more universal truth. Most parables have moral interpretations, inviting the mind to a consideration of virtue, responsibility, duty, and service. Some parables are descriptive of the condition of man, and like the emblem book of the Middle Ages, reveal the imperfection of man until human nature is united with divine nature.

In certain parts of the New Testament, Jesus is made to teach through parables, through homely sayings about familiar things. But the reader must not be deceived into overlooking the fact that a large part of the New Testament itself is a parable, a human statement of divine matters, and that Christ stands in the midst of the great Christian parable as the personification of the righteous man passing through the vicissitudes of life.

The Parable of the Talents

Matt. 25: 14-30 describes a certain man who calls unto himself his three servants, to the first of whom he gives five talents, to the second, two talents, and to the third, one talent. The first two servants increase their talents by trade, but the third buries him in the ground, and when the master returns from his journey he rebukes the third servant and takes from him the one talent that he has.

There are many interpretations of this parable, the most obvious of which is a statement of use, use or lose is a natural law. We are responsible for the abilities that we possess and are judged according to the application we have made of the knowledge that we possess. A man who possesses power and fails to use that power for the greatest good of all shall inevitably lose his power. A man of wealth who does not conscientiously administer the responsibility of wealth shall lose that which he has. It is the duty of all, that, possessing they share, knowing they teach, and commanding they serve.

A less obvious but more profound interpretation is suggested. The talents become like the mustard seed, a symbol of divine energies, or the doctrine, the teaching, the message Jesus Christ had to bring. Those who received to themselves this doctrine, were expected to go forth and increase the doctrine, thus fulfilling the responsibility of the learned. The man who hid his doctrine in the earth, that is attempted to hold truth and prevent others from receiving it, was rebuked by his master and lost the very wisdom he had attempted to keep for himself.

It is a common experience in religion to find a certain selfish desire to be superior. For example, I know of a certain case in which a student of the advanced philosophies secured a most precious book not generally available. The student desiring to keep the source of his new knowledge to himself, locked his book in the safe and refused to show it to others. Needless to say, he impoverished himself by his attitude and lost the very truth that he was seeking. A talent is not only a coin, it is a word that signifies an ability, some expertness or exceptional precocity. The parable can well be interpreted by regarding the talent as an enrichment of the soul, an ability to do something better than other men can do it. By this interpretation to hide one's talent is to lose it. It is expected of all men that they shall make use of the power which they possess, and again we must use or else lose.

In the parable, the servant who buried his talent in the earth, did so because he was afraid. He was a weak, conscientious man who believed that there was virtue in a conservative viewpoint. Here again the story urges man on to individual effort. It is not enough to possess, it is necessary to strive to make effort with possession, constantly to improve that which he has.

According to the Pythagoreans the soul of man is composed of eight parts. These parts are divided into three groups of which the first contains five, the second two, and the last one. These are termed Extensions of the soul. Here then is the true key to at least one esoteric interpretation of this parable. The first part of the soul is made up of the five senses, the media of cognizance. The second part of the soul is made up of the two principal body functions, nutrition and propagation. And the last or third part consists of one extension which is the physical body itself, the lowest extremity of the soul. The physical body then is the buried talent, buried not in earth but in the material sphere. The three servants, are the three parts of the soul, the divine, human, and animal soul. The master of the three servants is the spirit who truly is the keeper of the house. When man descends into a physical state and becomes conscious only of body and unaware of the spiritual parts of himself, he rightfully earns the displeasure of his master. A little consideration will clarify the entire parable.

THE PARABLE OF THE SEED

Mark 4 contains several parables of which two are important to our present consideration. The first is the Parable of the Sower: Some of the seed fell on stony ground, and some fell by the wayside to be devoured by the birds of the air, and some was scorched by the sun, and others fell among thorns, and a few fell upon good ground and brought forth a hundredfold. Christ explains the parable of the words of Mark 4: 14: "The sower soweth the word."

In this simple but truly inspired story is revealed the whole mystery of teaching. The sower is God, the seeds are truth, and the grounds into which they fall are the hearts of men. Some receive the truth and others reject it; some distort it, and others permit it to be plucked out by impulses and words; by weeds are to be understood the appetites and passions of the lower emotional nature; by the birds of the air, thoughts; by the sun, pride; and by the stony ground, such as are not yet ready to receive the law. But when the words of truth are brought to the one who is ready and in need, then it is said that the seed has fallen in good ground and from that heart grows up the tree of the soul, and truth increases like the mustard seed which being of no size in itself yet grows into a great bush, increasing many thousands of times.

In the heart of every man is the germ or seed of a divine nature. When it reaches the point of understanding, the seed is quickened and grows into a mighty tree, thus symbolizing the development of the whole spiritual nature, which increases greatly when man has learned to understand and obey the mysteries of the universe.

This is the key to the second parable, Mark 4: 26: "And he said, So is the kingdom of God, as if a man should cast seed into the ground." In the East it is taught that men are the harvest of the Gods. Man having received unto himself the divine power, increases as a plant and brings forth the flower and fruit. The fruit of the tree is wisdom, the perfect harvest of living; and the flower of the tree is virtue which gives way to wisdom. And it is the duty of man to become wise, even as it is the duty of the tree to bring forth fruit. As an old mystic of the Middle Ages once said: "Godliness is the fruit of life." The tree has always been the appropriate symbol of creation. To the Egyptians the universe actually is a tree; to the Norse people the magic ash Yggdrasill bore the world in its branches. The tree on Meru supports the heavens. Creation is a tree and man is the fruit of that tree. The whole visible cosmos conspires to perfect man who is truly the fruit of the tree of life. This parable is worthy of much meditation.

THE EYE OF A NEEDLE

The parable of the needle's eye occurs several times in the New Testament. Luke 18:25 contains the following statement: "For it is easier for a camel to go through a needle's eye, than for a rich man to enter into the kingdom of God."

In the wall of the ancient city of Jerusalem, there remains to this day a small door which is called the needle's eye. This gate is so narrow and low that for a camel to go through it, the animal must be unloaded. Thus, we have the key to the moralism of this parable. If the camel is relieved of its burden and lowers its head, it will just go through the Needle gate. In the parable, a rich man is one who possesses this world's goods, or more significantly, one who suffers from the illusion of the significance of this world's goods. A man may be poor and still have the rich man's curse, the desire for wealth, a complex of possessions, and impulse towards accumulations. As the camel must leave its burden behind if it would pass through the needle gate, so all men must leave behind the complex of accumulation if they would enter the kingdom of heaven. The spiritual sphere always is symbolized as having a tiny door that will just permit to enter what man is, but not what man has.

There is much misunderstanding on the subject of wealth and religion. There is no virtue in great wealth, nor again is their great vice if the wealth has been honestly accumulated. It is not what we have, but the consciousness of possession, the illusion that we may possess, that is the cause of difficulty. Man brings into this world nothing but what he is, and he takes from this world at the end, nothing but what he is. In the interlude between the cradle and the grave, men strive madly to accumulate the symbols of wealth and superiority. In their struggle to accumulate, these same men forget to become. The responsibility of possessions alone cramps the soul binding it Ixion like to the wheel of loss and gain. I have talked about philosophy to many people who have wealth; they always answer with a sigh:

"We should love to learn, but we are so hampered with the problems of the day and the administration of that which we possess."

Wealth, therefore, impoverishes man, deprives him of time, absorbs his interests, depletes his strength, and leaves him incapable of becoming wise. So, in the parable of the needle's eye, if we leave the burden behind, we may enter in. A man once asked Aristotle how much he wanted of this world's goods; and Aristotle replied: "Only this much, that if I fell into the sea, I could still swim ashore."

THE GOOD SHEPHERD

In Matt. 18: 12-13, is given the parable of the lost sheep. The shepherd leaving the ninety and nine sheep went forth to seek the one that had wandered away. In this parable, Christ is the psychopomp, the shepherd of souls. He is Anubis that guards the flock, the faithful one. He is Hermes, the herdsman, the keeper of the herds of heaven. He is Orpheus, the good shepherd. On the walls of the catacombs in Rome and the ruined villas of Pompei and Herculaneum are paintings of the good shepherd carrying in his one arm the sheep that had strayed and in the other the shepherd's crook, a hooked staff. On numerous occasions, Christ himself, identified with the lamb, is not only the shepherd but is also one of the sheep. He is the lamb of God. Those who accept him are purified in the blood of the lamb. He is a form of the scapegoat. To this day, his bishops carry the crosier to signify they are shepherds over men.

The interpretation of the shepherd's story is both moral and astronomical. Christ is a form of the sun-god, and like this solar deity sustains all life with his bounty. For the two thousand years prior to the Christian Era, and for several centuries thereafter, the vernal equinox occurred in the sign of the ram, the heavenly sheep. This lamb was the leader of the herd of constellations, the bellwether of the sky. It was for this reason that according to Godfrey Higgins in his Anacalypsis the priests of Eleusis came out on the portico of the temple at the time of the vernal equinox as early as 1400 B.C. and cried out to the assembled multitude as they held aloft a lamb: "All hail, Lamb of God that taketh away the sin of the world."

The shepherds so-called were the primitive initiates of those elder mysteries performed in remote ages. The wise man is a guardian of the flock of humanity. He leads his sheep into green pastures; he is the lawgiver, the priest, and the king, the ruler of the three worlds and of the three parts of man. Osiris, the Egyptian god of the underworld (the material sphere) frequently is depicted carrying the shepherd's crook. This same token of the shepherd was among the coronation scepters of the Egyptian pharaohs. When the mummified remains of Egypt's ancient kings are discovered by modern archeologists, the dried hands always hold the crosier, the symbol of temporal authority, and the fulfillment of the admonition: "Protect my sheep."

The sheep is an animal of gentle ways but no great brilliancy of mind. It always follows the leader and wails dismally if left behind. By this symbol is to be understood the great body of humankind which still follows the leader and wishes to be guided into green pastures. It is the duty of wisdom, of strength, and of integrity to guard the sheep. But there are false shepherds who would lead the sheep astray. And there are wild beasts that would carry away the lamb. So, the initiate teacher became the guardian of his disciples, protecting them against evil and leading them in the way of righteousness. The story is very old, part of the pagan symbolism of the ancient world. It has descended for nearly four thousand years, not as a Christian story, but as a story that has been Christianized because no more appropriate symbolism could be devised.

THE PEARL OF GREAT PRICE

In Proverbs 2: 2-5, it is written that wisdom is the most desirable of all things. She must be sought for as silver, and searched out as a hidden treasure. In Matt. 13: 45-46, is described the pearl of great price. This pearl is the kingdom of heaven. When a man discovers this pearl, he sells all his worldly goods that he may secure it, for it is valued above all other things.

The pearl is a most mysterious and sacred symbol, for it is produced within the oyster as a protection against some foreign substance that enters the shell. This is the same oyster described by Plato when he explains that man is held within his body, as an oyster is held within its shell. Man, through experience and suffering (the foreign particles) builds the soul (the pearl) as a protection or as a method of rendering evil harmless. The pearl thus becomes the symbol of the godliness and divinity that is within man, especially in its attribute as soul, the link between spirit and body.

During the medieval times there sprang up in Europe a mysterious sect called the Illuminate. The story of the pearl of great price became the most important part of their ritual, and members of the order were dedicated to the search for this pearl in the same way that the Knights of the Round Table sought for the Grail.

To the Illuminati, the pearl was a virtue, man's protection against evil; it was wisdom, man's protection against ignorance; it was faith, man's protection against death; and most of all, it was understanding, man's protection against life.

In the esoteric tradition, the pearl has gained a new, or rather a more perfectly stated meaning. The pearl of great price is hidden in the depths of the sea and those who would secure it must dive down into the waters and search for the pearl in the subaqueous sphere. Thus, the pearl becomes the symbol of truth; the ocean, the sea of rebirth; and the diver, the human spirit that must descend into the gloomy and mysterious depths in search of truth.

It is a proper part of symbolism that divine truths should find their analogies in the most precious of physical things. Thus, while base metals and nonprecious stones are the appropriate symbols of the physical world and its comparative unimportance, precious stones and the most valuable of the metals may be likened to spiritual matters. Therefore, the shrines of the gods are adorned with the most precious of this world's goods and the robes of the priests of ancient times were encrusted with jewels, and the ornaments of the temples were of the purest metal without dross. Man gave the best as his offering to the Best. Whatever was dear and valuable to him, was to some degree symbolical of truth, the most precious thing in the world.

In another parable, that of casting pearls before swine, the pearls become symbols of wisdom, and swine by their nature animals of gross and profane habits, that greater part of humanity which is incapable of comprehending wisdom. It is not right to profane wisdom by bestowing it upon that which obviously is unworthy. Wisdom must be superior, protected, and made available only to such as can comprehend it. That is why the esoteric sciences have remained, even to this day, in the possession of a few who bestow them only upon worthy and upright candidates. The Mysteries must not be defiled.

THE PRODIGAL SON

Luke 15: 11-32. The story of the prodigal son is the greatest of all the parables. It reveals an intimate knowledge of some of the deepest secrets of the pre-Christian mysteries and has become the inspiration of a vast literature.

It is the proper account of the fall of man. Goethe's Faust and Wagner's Parsifal are both based upon this fable. A son demanding his inheritance goes forth from his father's house and traveling to a distant land wastes his fortune in riotous living. Having lost all that he had, the prodigal who was reduced to the keeping of swine and to the greatest degradation, realizing at last the error of his way, returns to his father's house where his father receives him with great love and joy. A feast of welcome is prepared. The other brother who had remained honestly with the father was aggrieved that his prodigal brother should be preferred before him. The father explains that the one who went forth and returned again had been lost but had been found, which was an adequate reason for rejoicing.

The father's house, of course, is the divine world, the same father's house in which there are many mansions. The father himself represents God, and the two brothers two great waves of life. Of these, the prodigal son is humanity, and the righteous son who does not go forth represents the waves of life that never enter into a physical condition, that is never go down to Egypt, which in the Bible always represents a material and corrupted sphere. The son who went forth, descending into the material state, made numerous errors and misused the spiritual powers (wealth) which his father had given him. All the faculties and propensities of man are essentially divine, but material human beings have prostituted these powers and corrupted the spiritual virtues in the cause of material accumulation and power.

It is only after the unhappy experience of worldliness that man desires to return again to his father's house and begin the long and difficult evolutionary process which leads him back to God. At last, after numerous trials, he comes again to his father, who receives him with great joy and gives him preferment above his righteous brother, who never having been tempted had never risen above temptation.

In Parsifal, the drama is divided into three acts, the first of which is played in the castle of Mont Salvat, the temple of the grail which corresponds to heaven. The second act is played in the enchanted garden of Klingsor, the magician where the young knight Parsifal is tempted with all the illusions of flesh. This represents the distant country away from the father's house. The third act is also played in the temple of the Grail back on top of the mountain. Here is shown the return of the knight to his father's house.

The story of Faust is a little more complicated but it shows the same grand division. The first part is Faust's rebellion against the tyranny of scholasticism and learning. This corresponds to the young son desiring to go forth into the adventure of material existence. The second part, Walpurgisnacht, corresponds to Klingsor's garden, the inferior world with its temptations and perversions. The third part, called the redemption of Faust, proves "that a good man, even in adversity, shall not forget the God who let him be." Faust redeemed is lifted up amidst a chorus of angels.

The three parts of the story, therefore, are in terms of material evolution, involution, epigenesis, and evolution. That is the descent of consciousness into form, the tragic drama of consciousness in form; and the triumphant ascent of consciousness out of form. The story is again beautifully set forth in one of the most inspiring of the Gnostic poems, the hymn of the robe of glory.

THE BEGINNINGS OF THE CHRISTIAN CHURCH

A world religion always passes through certain mutations or phases before it becomes a widely recognized theological system. The founder of a great faith seldom lives to see his beliefs widely accepted. In the case of Buddha and Mohammed, however, the religion and its sects were well established in the lifetime of the prophets themselves. Religions are given to times and places. Jesus preached along the roads of Galilee. He preached to a people who had waited for centuries the coming of a Messiah. His voice was raised against the evils of his time and his scourge of small cords was for the corrupt of that day.

There is no reason to believe that Jesus previsioned the ages that were to come, the ages dominated by the letter of the law. He never saw the cathedral builders, the Templars, or the inquisitors.

The strength of the Christian revelation lay in the parables, the Sermon on the Mount, and the stories of the miracles. There is a body of obvious truths, of simple, direct, human truths, truths unchanged by time or empire. And around these truths was built up the great structure of Christian theology.

Then came interpretation, church councils and synods, the mumbling of profound mysteries, and balloting on the unity of God. Out of the chaos of the early councils emerged the churchianity of today. From this same source came such doctrines as vicarious atonement and infant damnation. From these synods came orthodoxy, the enemy of truth.

The modern agnostic, the modern skeptic, even the modern atheist, has small quarrel with the golden rule or the simple words of Jesus. Their bitterness is directed against the great institution that was built up about the life and words of one just man.

The occultist and the philosopher are entirely willing to accept the mystical truths of Christianity for they are a part of all truth, all revelation, and all mysteries. What the mystic seeks to escape is not true Christianity but the contending's of unnumbered jarring sects that have theologized Jesus out of existence and put in his place a figure of their own conception.

The philosopher is not anti-Christian, he is antitheological. He realizes that in the war of beliefs truth has been the victim of a conspiracy. The mystic believes with Dionysius the Areopagite that Jesus was a good man and that Christ was a mystery in the spirit. The struggle between these two beliefs, the humanity of Jesus and the divinity of Christ, is to be the subject of our next letter, to be titled THE JESUS OF PETER AND THE CHRIST OF PAUL.

Sincerely yours,

Manly P. Hall

Note: We deeply appreciate the kindliness and patience of those friends who have subscribed to our students' letters and have not yet received their complete series. Please accept our apologies for the delay and our assurance that the letters will be forthcoming as rapidly as possible.

AFTER READING THIS LETTER YOU WILL WANT THE WAYS OF THE LONELY ONES A COLLECTION OF MYSTICAL ALLEGORIES AND FABLES BY MANLY P. HALL. SIX FULL PAGE ILLUSTRATIONS. PRICE $1.50

LETTER NO. 11

Dear friend,

THE SECRET DOCTRINE IN THE BIBLE
THE JESUS OF PETER AND THE CHRIST OF PAUL

Several exceedingly difficult questions confronted the bishops and pastors of the primitive Christian Church. Most of these men were utterly unschooled in that pedantry which was later to bring confusion to Christianity. The faith of these first preachers of Christendom is not to be questioned. They bore ample witness to contrition and devotion. We shall, therefore, assume their absolute sincerity; but there is a vast gulf between sincerity and reason.

The early bishops were not theologians according to our present understanding of the word. They were pastors of small flocks. Some came from the deserts and others from the hills, a few from popular centers, but most of them from isolated communities. Courageous and contrite men, they desired to believe in the Christian dispensation, and the very desire gave substance to their beliefs. Such was the caliber of the men to whom the teachings of Christ had been entrusted by the apostles and disciples.

These ragged bishops, with their deacons and a few others, were elected to solve the mighty issues of the Church. Their words were to become dogmas, and even hasty utterances assumed canonical proportions. It would have been difficult enough if these devout but simple men had been confronted with profane matters. But these same men lay down their opinions on sacred and invisible matters beyond the ken of the most able jurist, though in a court of law their opinions would have had little weight.

Was Christ the Son of God or the son of man? Was he begotten of the Father or born in mortal wedlock? Was he identical with the Father? Did the Father give him dominion over all lands and all peoples? What was the Holy Ghost? Was Christ the same as the Holy Ghost? Were the Father, Son, and Holy Ghost one person, three persons, or one in three persons? It was also a mooted question as to whether divine unity was numerically or philosophically three. Was the Virgin Mary human or divine? Was it proper to worship, adore, or beseech the Virgin Mary?

These were weighty problems for illiterate men. Yet upon their decisions hung the future of a great religion and the fate of a thousand generations yet unborn. Is it to be wondered at that the bishops disagreed, that some were banished from the councils, and others branded as heresiarchs? Out of the struggles of these men after truth, out of their prayers and meditations, out of debate and controversy, out of feud and schism emerged Christian theology—the product of fallible men, dreaming after the infallible, seeking with finite minds to probe the mysteries of the infinite.

After they had finished their councils, the bishops and deacons returned to their deserts, their hills, and their towns, leaving behind them a monument of opinions which were to become the very essence of orthodoxy. From their groping's have emerged the hundreds of sects which together now constitute the Christian faith.

Broadly considered, these first bishops were divided into two camps, each ready to wage war upon the other. Nor did they ever become of one mind. From their synods and councils, held from time to time during nearly a thousand years, have emerged two utterly diverse opinions concerning the substance, nature, and estate of Jesus Christ.

To the first group, Jesus was a holy and good man, filled with the love of God. He had brought a revelation of the divine desire to his people. He was a patriarch like the holy ones of old, a prophet, a king of kings raised up among the Jews, a seer and a sage dignified above other men, because in his soul he had been lifted up into a communion with God. It was this doctrine of the humanity of Jesus that gave rise to Islamism. On one occasion Mohammed is reported to have said: "This Jesus was a good and holy man, a teacher among the Jews, but one day his disciples became mad and made a god of him."

To the second and favored group, whose opinion has long dominated the Christian Church, Christ was no ordinary mortal, but a very god incarnate, nominated and elected to this high estate by his own bishops. In Christ bodily dwelt the three persons of the godhead; in him dwelt the Creator of heaven and earth, wholly and completely. It was, therefore, the Sovereign Spirit of the world who walked beside the Sea of Galilee and preached from a boat beside its shore. God had taken on flesh and dwelt with men, had assumed the nature and appearance of a man, and had died crucified by his own creation. By his death the ever-merciful Father had opened wide the gates of salvation for all who believed in him.

These two utterly irreconcilable concepts were never to meet. Both survived, enduring to the present, each remaining as in the third century a thorn in the flesh of the other. Although Peter thrice denied his Lord, to him were given the keys of heaven. In the symbolism of Christianity, he was the "rock"—Petros, the stone on which the church of Christ was to be built. To Peter there were no "mysteries," all was literally and utterly true. Though the flesh sometimes failed him, Peter loved his Lord with a dogged devotion, content to follow after him, satisfied to be near him. To Peter, Christ was God, justified by the doctrine and demonstrated by the miracles. With an almost unlimited capacity to believe, Peter questioned nothing; and from his undoubting acceptance descended the Church of Christ, built upon his name, believing without questioning. To Peter, heaven and hell were places, and the middle distances of the world were filled with spirits, good and bad, herded by angels and demons.

Peter was not different from many of the evangelists of our present time who, in the face of an ever-growing knowledge, preach the "jot and tittle" of the scriptures. They demand that one accept the Bible as literal and unquestionable history. To them, it is an historical document. It never occurs to them that there might be something hidden in the "Book of books," some mystical and symbolical meaning that may only be recognized by an inner enlightenment quickened by the spirit. After nearly two thousand years, hundreds of millions of Christians today neither doubt, question, nor examine, but read, listen, and believe.

A very different kind of man was Saul of Tarsus—the little one—even in his own time a problem to the apostles. After his vision on the road to Damascus, Saul (who later became Paul) discovered the "mystery in the spirit." He possessed a peculiar advantage—he never had met Jesus and was not under the dominance of his powerful personality that seemed to control and blind the minds of the other disciples. Paul saw "as one afar off." He had a perspective that was absent in the others. Furthermore, he brought education and vision to the "mysteries" and discovered their inner meaning.

It was a task of early orthodoxy to confuse the Pauline epistles. Paul could not be ignored nor entirely destroyed. His sphere of influence had been too wide. The easiest solution was to corrupt his writings, thus destroying his subtler meanings. The result of this questionable strategy is obvious to the impartial reader. Paul is made to contradict himself; statements obviously inconsistent with his vision stand side by side with the most lofty and transcendental thoughts.

Mutilated though they be, the epistles of Paul reveal occasionally his mystical perception. Paul realized that it was not the Jesus who walked the dusty roads of Syria but the "Christ in you" that is the "hope of glory." He realized that Christ is a principle and not a man, that Jesus had come to "bear witness" for that principle. He had come to his own but his own had received him not. Paul sought to honor the teacher by honoring the teaching. He penetrated the outer veil of the temple before which the apostles knelt, and passed into the adytum where he beheld the "mystery" face to face.

Paul's larger story was the great problem of the early Church, and they sought in vain to confuse him. Paul knew the meaning of the mystical divinity, "the baptism of the Spirit." He realized that man must search vainly in the world for those precious spiritual truths that he can discover only within himself.

To Peter, the Christian "mystery" was that of God made flesh; to Paul it was flesh made God. These two could never mingle their interpretations into a common purpose, and it is recorded in the early writings that Paul visited Peter but Peter refused to see him.

Paul preached the Logos, that is, the teaching of the divine foundation of the world. Perhaps he was an initiate of some pagan "Mystery" resolved to "quicken" Christendom with the old truths. It is possible that he had contacted the germ of Gnosticism that had begun to unfold among the thinkers of Egypt and Israel. We cannot be certain of the source of Paul's knowledge, but one thing is true beyond doubt, Paul did know and his realization created a division within the Christian Church that all the centuries have been unable to overcome.

It is proper to study history but not proper to worship it. The Christian Bible is a semi-historical account of certain possible happenings which, in themselves, are not necessarily the appropriate foundation for a faith. Nor does this history, or neo-history, or in some cases outright fiction, insure salvation by the reading or acceptance of it. This is the error of the ages. In a desperate effort to preserve the "letter" of the law we have committed grievous errors in the name of truth.

By interpretation, we discover that Christianity is not the only religion to possess certain mystical traditions. The mystic cannot be creed-bound. If we search far enough into Christian metaphysics, we are apt to fall upon Greek and Roman pagan "mysteries" Buddhist philosophy, Pythagorean mathematics, and Gnostic ideology.

The fanatical attitude of the orthodox Christian historian is based upon the fear that a mystical interpretation will detract from the uniqueness of the Christian faith. To the individual who believes that Christianity is different from all other faiths, this would be a harrowing and mortifying discovery. It would breach the walls of Christian isolation, destroy forever the superiority complex of Christendom.

The attitude so far, therefore, has been, "It is better to see nothing rather than that which is not agreeable. Seek not lest ye find that which will compromise the sovereignty of Christian theology."

PAUL'S DOCTRINE OF THE LOGOS

There is every probability that Paul's conception of the divine "mystery" was profoundly influenced by Greeks philosophy. The New Testament was first written in Greek. The oldest existing manuscripts bear witness to Greek scholarship. There is no existing manuscript to indicate that the words of Jesus were first recorded in his own language.

At the beginning of the Christian Era, Greek scholarship dominated the Roman Empire. Roman patricians engaged Greek tutors for their sons. Rome—never a philosophical empire—dabbled superficially in Greek learning and then returned to its more congenial tasks of conquest and control. Many of the first converts to the Christian faith were men of Greek learning. Therefore, in the interpretation of Christian metaphysics, it will be useful to consider the substance of Platonic teaching concerning the nature of the Logos. It will then be obvious that the Christian teaching is but a thinly veiled restatement of the Greek original.

The god of the solar system was termed by the Greeks the Logos, or the Word—the same Word that, according to St. John, was made flesh. The Logos is three natures in one nature, the parts collectively being termed the Logoi. The divine nature in its own right is the First Logos. It is the One within whose nature all the parts of the solar system to the very circumference of the zodiac "live, and move, and have their (our) being."

From the nature of the First Logos is caused to emerge by will the Second Logos, which is the solar system in its visible parts—not born, but begotten, because it is the progeny of one nature. The First Logos is the invisible solar system, that is, the spiritual nature of the world. The Second Logos is the invisible made visible, the Word in its fleshly part. This Second Logos—generally termed the World—consisting of the planets, moons, and all the elements and creatures distributed throughout them, is truly the only begotten of the Father, consisting of a positive and a negative nature commonly known as spirit and matter.

The blending of spirit and matter produces form, and of all formal bodies the highest manifestation is mind. Therefore, Mind is the third person of the Logos, the Comforter, the Holy Ghost, the Seeker after divine "mysteries." Mind is that power within all objects existing in a temporal state which enables them ultimately to regain their invisible, divine condition through reason.

These three together—God, the Universe, and Mind—are the Three in One and the One in Three. These are the Logoi—the whole of Nature and its parts. The creating power abides in the midst of its world and is not manifested separately from it. Therefore, literally, Christ is the creation, the universe born of the invisible "mystery." It is obvious that the laws, principles, and forms of nature which make up the world could not be enclosed within the frail fabric of one mortal person, even should that person be an initiate of the highest order.

Jesus, then, is the one who bears witness. He must be regarded as a normal human being who, having discovered the "mystery," sought to incline men towards the attainment of the greatest good. He taught the multitude in parables, but to his disciples he told certain things not mentioned in the gospels.

It is quite possible that the great Gnostic book, the Pistis Sophia may be an account of the hidden doctrine which Jesus gave to his disciples. Of this we cannot be sure, but such is the claim that was made for the book by its original author in a time now remote.

The Pistis Sophia tells of the Aeon's and of the one who dwells in the light of the Soter, the son of the Aeon's—Truth—that shall save all who take shelter in it. Why more has not been heard of this book and the secret instructions which Jesus gave to Mary of Magdala is probably due to the cataclysmic effect its general circulation might have on Christian orthodoxy.

THE MARTYRDOM OF THE DISCIPLES

Nearly all the disciples of Jesus Christ are believed to have suffered martyrdom. The hagiology of the Christian Church describes in detail the suffering and death of the numerous martyrs of the early Church. In the Golden Legend, Jacobus de Voragine not only publishes exaggerated accounts, but, in his various descriptions of miraculous happenings, approaches the achievements of Baron Munchausen. It is natural, of course, that Christendom should revere its martyrs as noble men and women who had undergone the greatest trials and tribulations for their faith. Nor should any man be criticized or condemned for his belief and his willingness to die for it.

From an impersonal standpoint, however, the substantial facts are less colorful than one might imagine. Rome was exceedingly tolerant religiously. The temples of a score of faiths faced upon the Forum. As long as men paid their taxes and admitted their allegiance, Rome cared but little for private belief, provided that belief threatened no treason to the state.

During the imperial period, the Roman Caesars were regarded as proper objects of worship. Such worship, however, was not compulsory, and those who preferred to venerate Serapis, Osiris, or Xeus were free to do so. It was, however, a highly treasonable act to conspire against the station, person, or decrees of the Emperor, as these had a sanctity about them wholly inconsistent with the personal lives of the Caesars.

Impersonal consideration would indicate that very few of the first Christian martyrs were actually hilled for their beliefs. Most of them were arrested for sedition and executed for crimes against the solidarity of the state.

The apostate Emperor Julian—the noblest of all the Romans and a man of the highest personal integrity as well as a student of the deepest classical philosophies—sums up his dislike for the Christians, of which sect at one time he had been a member, simply and directly in better words than most of the other members were able to use.

Julian never was able to understand why the Christians had a special predilection for "sinners." The Church was apparently developing the idea that the worst sinner made the greatest saint. Julian regarded this attitude as highly detrimental to the state, because it encouraged delinquency by rewarding corruption instead of virtue. He also regarded as little less than seditious the Christian doctrine that all men are born sinners due to Adam's lamentable weaknesses. He also heartily disliked the political activity of various Christian groups, which were attempting to destroy by every possible means, perfidious or otherwise, the pagan Roman Empire.

He resented, furthermore, that a class of people within the boundaries of the empire, for the most part the poorest educated and of least estate, should fanatically expound a belief that they were the sole possessors of truth; that all other gods were demons; all other philosophers, frauds; and all other institutions, heretical. It is barely possible that the Emperor's annoyance was well founded. If the attitude of converts two thousand years ago resembled the attitude of certain modern Christian fanatics, one gains a greater degree of sympathy for the plight of the Romans who were having a faith thrust upon them without the right to say nay.

Once the prejudice against Christians had reached violent proportions, crimes were unquestionably committed against sincere and innocent people. One has only to consider the Inquisition to realize how the Christians themselves resented any imaginary or real interference with their own dogma. Christians have tortured more Christians and pagans for their beliefs than ever suffered martyrdom under the Caesars.

A religion to be secure, to be noble, to be truly sufficient must be established upon a great philosophy. It must appeal to both the reason and the heart. It must call to itself only the noblest and the best, and acknowledge as members only those whose virtues merit such inclusion. The Christian Church never did this or held these ideals, thus bringing much persecution upon itself, and also persecuting itself most gravely.

At the time of the introduction of Christianity, the Roman Empire was not in the state of corruption into which it afterwards fell as the result of internecine strife. The Romans celebrated the rites of Eleusis and of Dionysus derived from the Greeks. They performed, likewise, the rituals of Isis, Osiris, and Serapis, and they had begun to accept the Mysteries of Mithras, a Persian importation. The magnificent paintings which still survive upon the walls of the Villa of Dionysus at Pompeii prove beyond doubt that some, at least, among the Romans were true to the most enlightened Mysteries that the world has ever known.

Recent research is building up evidence to indicate that it was actually the Christians who burned Rome during the reign of Nero. The increasing body of archeological and historical material available today is reversing some of the opinions of the past. If it be true that Christian fanatics actually burned Rome, then the displeasure of the Romans and efforts to destroy the cult could hardly be regarded as persecution.

Fanaticism is a by-product of blind faith. When the emotions are stirred to an intensity of feeling and the mind is left unsatisfied or unfed, the result is frequently a form of hysteria or temporary insanity. This is the reason why it is so necessary to discover the true philosophical meaning beneath the Christian faith, so that intelligence may support belief and Christianity become a vital, living force in world affairs instead of a helpless observer of war and crime among men.

There are abundant indications of philosophical footings in the Christian religion. What is necessary is a general reform; new and complete translations of the Bible, with various possible alternative renderings, from the earliest Greek manuscripts; an admission that much is not known and not knowable; and, most of all, an attempt to reconcile Christianity with the great philosophies of the ancient and modern worlds rather than the preservation of an attitude of isolation. As long as there is fanaticism there will be martyrs. But other great philosophies have been promulgated without violence, because honesty of thinking appeals equally to all men.

Astronomy is one of the seven keys to the understanding of the New Testament. Relics of astrolatry (worship of the heavenly bodies) and cosmogony (consideration of the shape and order of the universe) are to be found in every important religious system. The twelve apostles of the New Testament are identical in meaning with the twelve jewels upon the breastplate of the high priest of Israel.

At some remote time, the zodiacal constellations were delineated among the star groups approximately paralleling the terrestrial equator. As these star groups do not resemble, in most cases, the creature or symbol assigned to them, the origin of the system must have been an arbitrary allocation according to laws of ancient theology. The Ptolemaic belief that the sun annually moved through the twelve signs of the zodiac, which were its many mansions, is frequently reflected in religious symbolism. Many medieval cathedrals throughout Europe are ornamented with zodiacal symbols, and in some cases these signs are actually associated with sacred persons.

It is exceedingly dubious that the original historical Jesus actually had twelve apostles. If he did by chance select this number, it was because he was aware of the astronomical significance. The destruction of numerous gospels after the Nicene Council indicates that many other apostles whose names have not survived may have been closely associated with the master and his work. The Church, however, following Egyptian and Greek precedent, arbitrarily fixed upon twelve, thus indicating that it was aware of the sanctity peculiar to this number.

In the astronomical symbolism, the sun entering into the various signs in sequence takes upon itself the phases, attributes, and aspects of those signs through which the solar force was said to be "mediated" or modified.

Therefore, the twelve disciples actually represent the twelve attributes of the Logos, or the sun, both visible and invisible, and should be considered the parts of one being rather than twelve separate beings, each with an arbitrary interpretation of its own.

When St. Augustine was asked why four of the apostles were especially designated from the rest, he replied that it was necessary that there be four principal gospels because there were four corners to the world, thus admitting a relationship between cosmogony and theology. The association of these four selected evangelists with certain creatures representing the four fixed signs of the zodiac intensifies the realization that we are dealing not with human beings but with the characters of a sublime cosmologic drama, reduced to human estate by the ignorance of clergy and laity alike.

Reference has already been made to the fact that the four gospels were themselves contrived, being merely accounts built up from material derived from the Gospel of Matthew. It seems, therefore, that it was necessary to make the four gospels so that the corners of the world would not be left without appropriate representation.

There is one other point of interest, in this connection. After the perfidy of Judas Iscariot, the number of the apostles was reduced to eleven. For this reason, St. Paul was added to the body of the elect to restore the perfect twelve. In spite of St. Augustine's opinion in allowing St. John to be assigned to the constellation of Scorpio, this arrangement was purely symbolical for astronomical purposes. In the original order Judas Iscariot was Scorpio. After his departure from the twelve, therefore, St. Paul assumes the toga of the Scorpion. The sign of Scorpio coincided with that season of the year during which initiation was usually given in the Greater Mysteries. Judas Iscariot is the negative Scorpio, unredeemed; St. Paul is the virtuous Scorpio, the enlightener, and of all the twelve, the most likely to have been an initiate of pagan Mysteries. It is, therefore, appropriate that the most important keys to initiation to be found in the New Testament should occur in the writings of Paul, the small one who had become great.

BEGINNING OF THE CHURCH

It is impossible to date with certainty the true time of the beginning of the Christian Church. It is only possible to specify the principal epochs within the structure of the Church itself. Christianity was punctuated by many councils that directed the whole movement of Christian theology.

Presumably, the Church began with Christ. There is no evidence, however, that the chief doctrines of the modern church, especially with regard to the sacraments, the nature of God, and so forth, were a concern of the first apostles. The Christian Church marched slowly over the background of its time, found increasing favor over a period of centuries, and with the death of Constantine became the ruling power in ecclesiastical Europe.

It has been said that Jesus gave the doctrine and Constantine gave the church. This approximately summarizes the matter. The power of the early Church lay in its influence over the masses. It was not the faith of the noble during the first centuries but the faith of the shopkeeper and even the slave. Its power increased through the sheer weight of numbers rather than through special favor by any group. Its early dogmas were uncertain; there was much groping. But after the Council of Nice, a certain integration was obvious, and this was the true foundation of the Church. The ante-Nicene period was the period of apology. The great fathers of this time were engaged upon a defensive program. The heathen and the infidel were appropriately stigmatized; but loudest of all, arose the cry to be heard and to be given an opportunity to prove the magnificence of the new religious ideal. A number of the old pagans were treated not only with tolerance but with generosity. Hermes met with the approval of the fathers, and Plato's teachings were given considerable attention.

After the Nicene Council, apology gave place to diatribe. The early Church was more sure of itself. It no longer asked, it demanded. The post-Nicene fathers proclaimed their opinions, whereas earlier writers had advanced theirs with caution.

The post-Nicene fathers also had a quicker eye for heresy. A mass of belief was gradually being shaped into a creed to which there must be conformity. There was some confusion in the effort to determine fine points of acceptance or rejection, but the faith was strong with youth and began the moral conquest of Europe, a course which remained unchecked until the Reformation.

The Christian Church occupied a unique position in the policies of medieval Europe. It was a sovereignty unto itself, demanding allegiance from all sovereigns. It regarded itself as the ultimate empire, above and beyond all temporal purpose or power. Kings sat upon their thrones because of the favor of the Church, and at the dictates of the Great Mother, king and commoner alike must act.

The Reformation brought to an end the Church's dream of temporal power. One after another the Protestant sects broke away. The Church thundered in vain. Men lost faith with their spiritual leaders because of the numerous occasions on which certain dogmas of theology had been proved fallible. The result is a Christendom divided against itself.

What brought about this great change?

In the first place, after the birth of science, man became more and more conscious of his physical estate. In earlier days, physical security was unknown. Plague, pestilence, and war destroyed him. Life was short and the struggle difficult. Printing brought him books, and books brought with them education. Man became aware of the outer world. He lived no more merely in the anteroom of heaven, but in a spacious physical universe in which there was room and opportunity for physical achievement. The Church had taught that material life was nothing, that man should be constantly preparing himself for eternity. Exploration enlarged the world. The invention of the telescope and the microscope made man matter-conscious. He saw his physical life as significant and he dreamed of schemes to lengthen it. He sought wealth and position, and refused to continue to regard himself as a sinner merely through the accident of existence. The more he lived in the physical world the more distant the invisible world became, and by the middle of the nineteenth century it focused his attention so completely upon matter that he came even to doubt the existence of those very demons who had plagued his forbears. Thus, released and removed from bondage to invisible things that once he had worshipped, theology ceased to fascinate him.

This great swing of the pendulum was the inevitable consequence of fanaticism. From one extreme the mind moves inevitably to the other. The pendulum swings eternally from God to godlessness, and back again. As from some strange, fantastic prison man has emerged from theological domination. Having breathed the atmosphere of freedom of thought, he regards as the most cherished possession of life the right and privilege to order his life by the light of individual reason.

Yours sincerely,

Manly P. Hall

LETTER NO. 12

Dear Friend,

THE SECRET DOCTRINE IN THE BIBLE
THE REVELATION OF ST. JOHN

It was the wish of Martin Luther that the Book of Revelation should be omitted from his translation of the Bible. In his opinion, the Apocalypse was of pagan origin and was not a writing of the beloved John. It was filled with Hermetic inferences and strange allegories which troubled the soul of the great German reformer. Though not greatly learned in comparative religion, Luther sensed the Gnosticism that pervaded the book. He denied the divine inspiration of the entire work, affirming with Erasmus that the Apocalypse had no legitimate place in the Christian scripture. He raised his voice against tradition, but tradition stronger; and after his death, the Book of Revelation was restored to the Bible and has remained in its accustomed place ever since.

The debate concerning the origin of the Book of Revelation began in the second century. Even the Gospel according to St. John was involved. Dionysius of Alexandria declared that both books had been written by Cerinthus, a Gnostic, who, to add credence to his writings, had appended thereto the name of John. Later, St. Jerome attacked the validity of the Apocalypse, lending to the controversy one of the greatest names in the Church. Jerome insisted that through some machination of the evil one, the devil had introduced his voice into the scripture itself in an effort to undo the whole labor of Christendom.

It must be acknowledged, then that the authorship of the Revelation is extremely uncertain. The claims of the Authorized Version that it was the work of John while on the Isle of Patmos may be liberally discounted. It is quite possible that the Cerinthus story is the correct one. If so, the Revelation may be the most important work in the entire New Testament for the reason that it arose from Gnostic scholarship.

From a philosophical standpoint, the Book of Revelation exhibits a wisdom far in excess of the other Testament writings. Here comparative religion is introduced. The great mystery institutions which dignified the past with their initiates find a place in the Apocalypse. The rites of Phrygia, those celebrating the Aged One who walks amidst the lamps; the rites of

Osiris wherein are set forth the last judgment; and the rites of the ancient sun-god and the horsemen who ride through the sky; all these, and many others, are to be found set forth in various sections of the Apocalypse.

Recent translations of Egyptian manuscripts indicate that in some cases the pre-Christian text has been quoted word for word. Here indeed is the mystery of pagan books, with only the change of an occasional thought or word, wandering into the Christian scriptures, becoming canonical, and remaining century after century unidentified as to their original sources. John was one of the disciples who did not suffer martyrdom. He is believed to have been buried at Ephesus, the city of the Mysteries, near the tomb of the Virgin Mary, John sleeps through the centuries, awaiting the return of his Lord. When that great day comes, he will arise and be seated upon the right side of his master.

These legends have little regard for history, but are products of the traditional trend in early Christian thought. During this period, fantastic accounts of Christian origins were developed, and these inventions ultimately took on a stature second only to the scriptures themselves. There was a wild confusion of Christian and pagan doctrine. The Greek god Dionysus was canonized, as was also his Roman mode, Bacchus. The pagan mathematician Hypatia, a victim of Christian monks, blossomed forth as St. Catherine of Alexandria. It was not until the end of the Dark Ages that anything resembling reason could be clearly distinguished in the picture. This was no time of critical scholarship. From our present perspective, it is reasonably certain that the Apocalypse is a compilation of pagan doctrines with an occasional Christian reference interpolated into the text.

Revelation 1:9 reads: "I John, who also am your brother, and companion in tribulation, and in the kingdom and patience of Jesus Christ, was in the isle that is called Patmos, for the word of God, and for the testimony of Jesus Christ."

During the years when John is supposed to have lived on the Island of Patmos, he was far from the boundaries of Christian influence. The people who dwelt in that region were called Priscillianists, the followers of a priestess by the name of Priscilla. She was similar to the Roman sibyls, practicing strange rites and giving oracles.

The Priscillianists borrowed from the Gnostics and the Manicheans, and from the wild diffusion of doctrines, conceptions, and sorceries that were practiced at Patmos, Ephesus, and Philadelphia. They observed nocturnal rites in grottoes and caverns. They believed in a messianic tradition and preserved their mysteries under what were called Phrygian rites.

The Phrygian Mysteries were celebrated not only near Patmos but at Ephesus and Philadelphia, two of the seats of the early Church. The Phrygian arcana were a curious combination of the messianic tradition of Egypt, part of the Dionysian Mysteries of the Greeks, together with elements from the Mithraic doctrines of Persia. It was a conglomerate mysticism which grew up and flourished in the most polyglot areas of the Near East, especially at Ephesus which was called the melting pot of the ancient world.

Ephesus has been referred to as the "city of the sorcerers." Caravans of traders came there from all parts of the then known world to exhibit their wares. A score of strange religious beliefs and rites mingled, mixed, and prospered in the confusion of the community. Devotees worked spells and enchantments; black magic, necromancy, and divination throve in the congenial atmosphere. The concourse abounded in witches and magicians who sold indiscriminately love potions and poison.

And over this bustling community brooded the sovereign goddess, Diana of the Ephesians.

It should not be concluded, however, that Ephesus was without genuine enlightenment in spiritual matters. Here Buddhist thought mingled with Greek, and the religions of the corners of the earth found common meeting ground. The result was a broader and more tolerant learning than would have been natural in a more secluded area. It was because of this cosmopolitan atmosphere that the Apocalypse contains such a wide distribution of ideas. The book could not have been the product of one simple Syrian. It required a broad contact with the beliefs of the time, and an acquaintance with many forms and styles of learning.

The rites of Phrygia included much of Sabeanism or astrolatry. The initiates worshipped the sidereal bodies and various celestial phenomena. The ancients had conceived the symbol of a ladder leading upward from the earth to heaven. This is Jacob's ladder, and the ladder of Mithras. In his "Cave of the Nymphs" (a fragment from the wanderings of Ulysses). Homer describes a sacred cavern of Zarathustra. He says that the cave represents this world. There are two great arched doorways, and the ceiling is painted to represent the heavens. Of the two entrances, one is for the descent of souls, and the other for the return upward of the "gods" to the celestial state.

Revelation 4:1 reads: "After this I looked, and, behold, a door was opened in heaven: and the first voice which I heard was as it were of a trumpet talking with me; which said, Come up hither, and I will shew thee things which must be hereafter." This verse must be interpreted according to the doctrines of the ancient pagans. The door which opened in heaven is one of the two gates of the mundane sphere. John ascended a symbolical ladder composed of the seven churches, not to be considered literally as religious institutions, but as symbols of the rungs of the ladder of the Mysteries. Even Tertullian and Epiphanius acknowledged that there were not the seven churches at the time of St. John.

The nature of the ascent into the mystery of divine things is clarified further in the opening words of Revelation 4:2: "And immediately I was in the spirit." This can only mean an illumination or internal spiritual mystery by which John was raised up through the door in the mundane sphere into communication with that which abode above the firmament.

Having ascended by a mystical experience, John is made to describe symbolically that which is above the material heavens. He saw a throne, and upon the throne was a great light. Before the throne were four and twenty elders and seven lamps; and the throne was surrounded with a great sea of glass like crystal.

The interpretation is Gnostic. The throne and he who sat upon it represents the lord of the mundane states, Ildabaoth [Yaldabaoth] master of the Aeon's. About him are the symbols of the hours which make up time. And before his throne are the lights which are his children, for it is said that from the lord of the Aeon's came forth the princes of the seven planets.

The sea like crystal is the waters which are above the firmament as described in Genesis 1:7. This superior sea is described by Socrates who declares that there are creatures which dwell about the shores of the air which are imperceptible to men. This is the Schamayim of the Cabala, the sideral sea that washes the shores of heaven. This also is the proper sea of life, the waters of life, the heavenly humidity, the ocean of generation, from which souls, once immersed in its mysterious essence, fall into the sphere of generation. It is described in detail in the Divine Pymander of Hermes and in the writings of the Neoplatonists. In every great system of mythology, this superior sea is mentioned. It is this same water which is above the firmament which is supposed to have descended in the flood of Noah. In the mystery of initiation, this sea becomes a laver of purification, and as such was symbolized in the rites of the tabernacle by a fountain or basin in the courtyard, with its surface inlaid with the mirrors of the women of Israel.

The section of the Apocalypse which deals with the seven lamps in the midst of which walks the Ancient One is pure Sabeanism. The seven golden candlesticks are the seven planets, and he who walks in the midst of them is the same as the mysterious being who is seated on the throne above the heavens, and the shining figure that rides upon the wheels and the cherubim in the vision of Ezekiel. He wears a golden girdle, his hair is as white as snow, his eyes are as a flame of fire, his feet are like brass, and his voice as the sound of many waters. In his right hand he holds seven stars, and from his mouth comes forth a sharp two-edged sword.

Even the wildest imagination cannot construe this figure to be an orthodox part of Christian theology. He wears the attributes of the seven powers of God, and, according to Revelation 1:20, the stars in his hand are the angels of the seven churches. He is garmented in white and like the great figure of the Zohar, moves in a splendor perceptible only to the awakened eye of the seer.

And what are the seven churches which are in Asia? They are the seven races, the seven continents, the seven days of creation, the seven sacraments, and the seven mysteries. They are the seven vowels which are spoken by the mouth, the seven senses of the perfect mm, the seven bodies of the complete man, and the seven principal orifices of the body.

The mystery of the seven is the supreme mystery of the one who was, is, and shall be, Ildabaoth, lord of the Aeon's, creator of all forms in the mundane sphere, ruling like Zeus with a sevenfold scepter of universal law. He is the master of the Mysteries, hierophant of the rites of Phrygia, keeper of the seven keys by which shall be opened the seven doors of the Mysteries. The mystery of the seven is completed in the story of the seven seals and the seven churches. The churches constitute a ladder, the lowest rung of which is the symbolic church of Ephesus. Ephesus was ruled over by Diana, a lunar goddess. Therefore, the order ascends from the moon to Mercury, the church of Smyrna; then comes Pergamos, the church of Venus; Thyatira, the sun; Sardis, Mars; Philadelphia, Jupiter; and lastly, Laodicea, Saturn. There are other arrangements assigning the churches differently to the planets, but the result in each case is the same; the churches are rungs of the ladder which leads upward from the elements to the stars.

Astronomically considered, the vision of John assumes unexpected significance. Ascending through the door in heaven, he beholds the constellational diffusion composed of the twelve northern constellations and the twelve southern constellations. These were called the associates or the First

Army of the Redeemed. The northern constellations were called the northern brethren, and the southern constellations the southern brethren. Each was crowned to represent the fact that it was a radiant star or star group.

The ancients considered the area south of the equator as a great ocean from which the constellation arose. The great monster or leviathan creeping out of the southern sea was, therefore, Cetus, the constellation of the whale. This had been related earlier in the story of Jonah. It is interesting to note that the round table of King Arthur contained space for twenty-four Knights seated before panels alternately black and white.

At the beginning of the present astronomical age, there was a conjunction of the seven planets in the sign of Aries. This is described in Revelation by the symbol of the lamb with seven eyes and seven horns. By eyes must always be understood planets or stars, and by horns, the power or ray which emerges. In modern astrology, the sun is exalted in the sign of the ram. Bacchus is pictured in the ancient mosaics with a lamb in his arm, and in the catacombs of Rome, figures believed to be those of Christ carry the lamb in one arm and hold the shepherd's crook in the other hand. Jesus is referred to as the good shepherd. Hermes was the shepherd of souls, master over the little stars of the constellation of the ram. The sun is essentially dignified n Leo and exalted in Aries, therefore it is written: "The lamb and the lion shall lie down together."

It is usual to represent the Book of Revelation as a scroll from which are suspended seven seals. These seals represent a mystery, a secret which cannot easily be revealed because it is sealed up in the mysteries. By the seals is also to be understood the seven keys of the scriptures by the possession of which the initiate may behold all mysteries and all ruth. Upon the opening of the first seal, a horseman rode forth upon a white horse. Revelation 6:2: "And he that sat on him had a bow; and a crown was given unto him: and he went forth conquering, and to conquer." Here, again, is the moon and the bow of Diana.

When the second seal was opened a red horse came forth; and he who rode upon the horse was given a great sword to take peace from the earth. The second horse and rider represent the sun.

Upon the opening of the third seal, a black horse came forth; and he who sat upon the horse had a balance in his hand. Revelation 6:6: "And l heard a voice in the midst of the four beasts say, A measure of wheat for a penny, and three measures of barley for a penny; and see thou hurt not the oil and the wine." Oil and wine represent soul and spirit, and the barley and wheat, the lower nature of man. The destroyer upon the blacky horse is Saturn.

The fourth seal, when it was opened, gave forth a pale horse, and the name of him that sat upon it was Death, and hell followed with him. The pale horse is Venus; and Venus is Lucifer, the rebel angel whose light was taken from him.

The fifth seal is the seal of the martyrs who cried out in a loud voice. Revelation 6:10: "How long, O Lord, holy and true, dost thou not judge and avenge our blood on them that dwell on the earth?" The fifth seal is Mars, the seal of blood.

The sixth seal, when it was opened, gave forth a great earthquake, the stars fell from the heavens, the sun became black, and a great and mighty motion moved the heaven and the earth, and the kings of the earth hid themselves. The sixth seal is Jupiter.

The seventh seal was called the great silence, and out of the silence at the sounding of the trumpet of the seventh angel appeared a mystery called the "woman clothed with the sun" who was bearing a man child. This seventh seal is Mercury which completes the great vessels of wrath.

When the seals were opened, the power of them fell upon the earth and upon all natures, therefore, these modes of energy were represented as seven vials which poured out their contents upon the world.

The story of the woman clothed in the sun who went forth into the wilderness to give birth to her child is susceptible of a most prophetic interpretation. About the time of the beginning of the Christian Era, the temple at Jerusalem was destroyed and the Alexandrian libraries were burned. Wisdom departed into the desert where it was cultured and guarded by the Arabs for nearly a thousand years, and then returned again to Europe by way of Moorish Spain. Astronomically speaking, the woman clothed with the sun is the position of the sun in Virgo which corresponds with the present Catholic feast of the Assumption of the Virgin in which she is lifted up in glory with her Son.

The last judgment is derived almost completely from the metaphysics of Egypt. According to the Egyptians, the human being is born with seven souls which are in a way the potential powers of the seven planets in man. The souls are manifested through the seven senses, the seven vital organs, and the seven bodily systems. Each of the seven souls has its planetary name. Saturn is the contemplative or rational soul; Jupiter is the reasonable soul; Mars is the impulsive soul; the sun is the vitative soul; Venus is the amative soul; Mercury is the intellectual soul; and the moon is the vegetative or generative soul.

The seven souls together are the bodies of a self which is the ruler of the entire bodily economy. These souls may be lost, one or more of them, by the misuse of the qualities which they represent. In the Book of the Dead, papyrus of Ani, the spirit of the deceased, speaking from the urn of the heart, beseeches Osiris: "Let me not perish with the king that ruleth for a day." This is the personality. In each life we have a personal complex which is a king ruling for a day. After death the complex is broken up and the seven souls return to the seven planets unless initiation has bound them together in a spiritual personality.

In the great hall of Amenti, in the room of the columns of the twin truths, the beam and the balance were set up for the last judgment. The twelve assessors (modern jury derived from this) were seated to decide the verdict. Thoth, Lord of the Writing Tablet, prepared to set down the findings. Anubis, the jackal-headed, brings in the heart of the departed, whose Ka or ethereal self is also present to behold the judgment. Osiris enthroned, his body filled with eyes, presides over the weighing. The crocodile-headed Set waits to devour the heart of the unworthy; and Cynocephalus, the ape of wisdom, sits on the beam of the balance. The feather of Maat is placed upon the scales and soul is weighed. If the deceased is perfect in the negative confession of faith (7 have not committed, etc.) it goes forth into the plains of Aaru where the "reeds are long" and there is happiness for the day that has no night.

If the seven souls are lifted up, they become a seven-headed creature, but those parts which fail are judged unworthy of the resurrection, and are cast into darkness. The outer darkness represents the various planes of the universe from which these souls have come. Here each disintegrates into its primal substance, resulting in the picturing of the seven hells. But it is not the spirit that goes to these places of punishment, but the castoff souls which are slowly destroyed and their essences returned to the planes from which they came.

The psychostasia or weighing of the soul has been taken bodily from the Egyptian rites and, with only a few interpolations and changes, has been made the last judgment of Revelation. The dead who rise from their graves at the sound of Gabriel's trumpet is a mystery of initiation. They arise not from the earth, but from their bodies into the spiritual state. The New Jerusalem consummates the mystical drama. Here is the city four square, its gates and walls of jewels, adorned as a bride. The New Jerusalem should not be regarded as a city, or even as a symbol of a place.

The New Jerusalem is the perfected and redeemed measure and proportion of the initiate. He himself is a sanctified and holy place adorned as a bride.

It was an early Christian custom for those entering sacred orders to be united by a mystical marriage with Christ. They, indeed, were the "brides of the lamb." As a whole, the church itself theoretically was a bride ready to be united with truth, to be lifted up into holy communion with the most high.

The New Jerusalem is not lighted by the sun nor by the moon, but the lamb is the light thereof. Its jeweled foundation is the breastplate of the old tabernacle. It is St. Augustine's City of God. According to the Platonists, those who had received the Mysteries, that is, according to Christendom had been taken into the Ecclesia, were as a race apart. The old pagan dialogues describe the sages who meet in their groves far from the abode of men and here reason together upon the mysteries of the universe. The New Jerusalem, therefore, is the temple of the greater Mysteries, the house built without the sound of hammer or the voice of workmen, which is eternal in the heavens. It is the city of the Son existing in the paradisiacal sphere from which man fell in the book of Genesis.

According to Jacob Boehme, the New Jerusalem is the redeemed Adam, the man lifted up by the mystery of Christ. It is, therefore, a spiritual symbol of a mystical state of being where those dwell together who have received the light.

In the parable of the prodigal son is described a man who went from his father's house and wasted his substance among the fleshpots of Egypt. He then became a keeper of swine, less than the least. But after these sad adventures he returned to his father's house, sadder but wiser, and rejoiced to remain there. In the Hymn of the Robe of Glory, a Gnostic fragment, is set forth the story of one who travelled far and forgot the land from which he came. As he wandered among the bazaars and shops of Egypt, he found no happiness or satisfaction, for dimly through his forgetfulness, he sensed his participation in some other life long forgotten. In the grail legends, there is the story of Parsifal, the guileless fool, who having entered the castle of the grail, there beheld a great mystery which was beyond his understanding. He, therefore, was sent forth again into the world; and after grievous sufferings, he again discovered the castle of the grail. All these stories have an identical meaning. Like the Odyssey of Homer, they describe the wanderings of the soul in search of "its own far distant land."

In the Apocalypse is set forth a strange, fantastic pageantry, the story of the Mysteries. It seems as though the book had been taken bodily from some learned and ancient rite. It is the only book that has descended to us in which the rituals of the Mysteries are openly described. The study of it must completely change the Christian viewpoint. The understanding of it must bring a universal perspective wider far than the corners of Christendom.

CONCLUSION

It is impossible in a few hundred pages to interpret the mysteries of the Old and the New Testaments. All that we can do is to remind each and every Bible student that there is a mystery, not apparent to the mind alone, nor the reason, but a mystery that must be experienced inwardly through realization. Historically the Bible is of little value. Its literary excellence comes not from the original, but from repeated reediting to match the scholarship of the times. Its strength lies in its presentation of the Mystery teaching of ancient Israel and early Greece. It is a book of comparative religion and worthless to the individual who perceives Christianity to be a unique revelation. It is read weekly by the thousands of churches of Christendom, but remains sealed with its seven seals until the individual seeder opens it with his own scholarship and understanding.

The first step must be a serene tolerance, even better, a sublime realization that the Mysteries of God have been given in all time to all peoples according to their capacity to understand. If you would read the Bible intelligently, you must read certain commentaries by which its keys are made to turn in the ancient lock. The following are some of the most important commentaries:

The Six Books of Proclus on the Theology of Plato translated by Thomas Taylor. London, 1816.

The Gnostics and their Remains by C. W. King. London, 1887. Pistis Sophia translated by G. R. S. Mead. Theosophical Publishing Society, London, 1896.

The Book of Beginnings by Gerald Massey. London, 1881.

The Natural Genesis by Gerald Massey. London, 1883.

Egypt the Light of the World by Gerald Massey. London, 1907.

The Ghebers of Hebron by Samuel Pales Dunlap. New York 1898.

The Historical Library of Diodorus the Sicilian. Diodorus Siculus. Various translations.

The Book of the Dead. Various translations.

The Jewish Wars by Josephus. Various translations.

The Mishna. Various translations.

The Babylonian Talmud.

The Jerusalem Talmud.

Sepher Ha Zohar.

Sepher Yetzirah: The Book of Formation and the Thirty-Two Paths of Wisdom. Translation by Wm. Wynn Westcott. Theosophical Publishing Society, London, 1893. Translation by Knut Stenting. Wm. Rider & Son, London, 1919.

The Guide for the Perplexed, by Moses Maimonides. Translated from the original Arabic text by M. Friedlander. E. P. Dutton and Co., New York 1919.

The writings of St. Chrysostom.

The writings of Origen.

All of these works are available in English; many can be secured from your own library, or borrowed by your library from the Library of Congress for your use. Through an understanding of the origins and developments and the beliefs relevant to Christianity, it is possible to understand at least in part the Gnostic Mysteries in the New Testament. You will also gain some insight into the changes and interpolations which have been made, and so have crippled the text.

It is not merely a desire for scholarship that should impel this research, but rather a desire for understanding and a true insight into the mysteries of the scriptures. The Holy Bible is the sacred book of Christendom, the spiritual guide of nearly 800 million people. A work so widely diffused throughout human society and so intensive a part of the lives of human beings should be read with understanding, with some grasp of the broader meanings and deeper inferences. Superficiality has led to intolerance, but depth of scholarship will bring about an adequate tolerance.

We should remind you that other peoples also have their sacred books, writings which have guided moral conduct and spiritual aspirations for centuries. These scriptures of non-Christian peoples should receive the same veneration and the same research that is accorded to our more familiar writings. All the Bibles of the world united together reveal one spiritual tradition. They all bear witness to an enlightenment which is imperishable and which has been passed on from age to age as a priceless heritage of wisdom. Every person who is a student of the Christian Bible should read the principal non-Christian scriptures, not critically to point out their defects, but with a sincere desire to increase his own knowledge through a wider acquaintance with the inspired writings.

In the last twenty-five years there has been a considerable breaking down of religious prejudices. The sacred books of other peoples are now available to all who desire to read them. Read first the Koran, its inspiration seated in the Christian Revelation; then the Dhammapada, the great Buddhist scripture of the Law; then some small section of the Indian writings such as the Bhagavad Gita. From that pass to the Chinese; read the great Confucian classics, and Lao-tse's Toa Teh King.

When you have made this brief survey, ask yourself sincerely if each of these sacred books has not added something to your inspiration, or clarified some point of spiritual conduct. In a world torn by materialistic beliefs, these noble and inspired writings give added courage to meet the problems of the day.

Examine several editions of the Christian Bible, as for example, compare the King fames version with the modern revised edition and a recent publication The Bible as Living Literature. Consider the polyglots, and get a parallel Greek-English text. You will make many interesting discoveries. You will find that upon the skeleton of the Greek text has been built the beautiful version that we know. We will discover numerous errors and alternative renderings, and slowly recover from the infallibility complex from which so many orthodox Bible readers seem to suffer. Read the Vulgate, the Septuagint. And get a good dictionary of English-Hebrew terms. These will all prove valuable. They will not destroy your faith in the Bible, but they may injure your faith in some of its translators. You will see the uselessness of picking phrases to pieces and trying to think in terms of "jots and tittles." You will be free to consider the larger issues.

The Christian Bible as we know it today is a fragment of the Christian traditions of the first and second centuries. This fragment was arbitrarily preserved and the rest destroyed. Politics and policy played a large part in the compilation. Still, with all its faults, and with all its misinterpretations, the Christian Bible is the greatest book m English literature. But like most other great books, it must be approached with understanding, gentleness, impersonality, and a sincere desire to find truth.

Sincerely yours,

Manly P. Hall

AUTHOR AND MANAGING EDITOR

Darrell Jordan is an acolyte of the August Fraternity, former Noble Grand-IOOF and Freemason. He is also a member of the Theosophical and Philalethes Societies.

Darrell Jordan

BOOKS BY THE AUTHOR

- Illustrations of Masonry
- Surviving Document of the Widow's Son
- The Undiscovered Teachings of Jesus
- The Initiates
- Jefferson's Bible
- Master Masons Handbook
- Forgotten Essays - W.L. Wilmshurst
- Forgotten Essays - Waite
- Forgotten Essays - H. Stanley Redgrove
- The Writings of Sigismond Bacstrom M.D.
- Forgotten Essays – Reincarnation
- Masonic Writings of George Oliver
- Masonic Lectures by Wellins Calcott
- The Fellowcraft Handbook
- Secret Societies
- Vibration and Life
- Key to the Rosicrucian Characters
- The Revelation of John
- Life and the Ideal
- The Philosophical History of Freemasonry
- The Magic of the Middle Ages
- Musings of a Chinese Mystic
- The Life of the Soul
- Christian Mysticism
- Krishna and Orpheus
- The Eleusinian Mysteries & Rites
- The Crucifixion Letter
- The Mystic Key
- You Paid What?
- The Illustrated Pioneer History of the America
- Montana Freemasons 19th Century
- Washington Freemasons 19th Century
- Idaho Freemasons 19th Century
- Rock Metaphysics
- Emblems: Jean Jacque Boissard and Otto van Veen
- Emblems: Nicholas M. Meerfeldt
- Alchemy Art: Manly P. Hall
- Emblems: Manly P. Hall
- Alchemy Art & Symbols
- Splendor Solis

For the latest information, please visit author's book site: Parallel47North.com/collections/esoteric-books

If you have any question, suggestion, or feedback, please contact:

info@Parallel47North.com

MANLY P. HALL BOOK SERIES

All Seeing Eye Book Series

A Seeker of More Intelligent Life Book Series

Hand-drawn Illustration of Manly P. Hall and Book Cover Art by Jessica Naomi.

The Artist Portfolio: JessicaNaomiDesigns.com

www.ingramcontent.com/pod-product-compliance
Lightning Source LLC
Chambersburg PA
CBHW020310010526
44107CB00001B/47